100 Days of Table Tennis

By Coach Samson Dubina
www.samsondubina.com
©2015
v06-26-15
All Rights Reserved

On the Cover: Coach Samson Dubina in Action
Photo Credits to CLJ Studios, SwanShot.com, Heather Dubina,
Pierce Scott, Profusion Productions, and Barry Carlin
Bible quote NKJV

Edited by Larry Hodges

Cover design by Simplex Creative.
Online portfolio at www.simplexcreative.biz

Introduction 6

Preface…………………………………………………….…7

Chapter 1 ...... **Beginnings** 8
    Day 1 .... Basic Principles of Table Tennis 9
    Day 2 .... Writing Out of a Game Plan 11

Chapter 2 ...... **Strokes** **15**
    Day 3 .... Body Position 16
    Day 4 .... Serve 17
    Day 5 .... Drive 18
    Day 6 .... Push 19
    Day 7 .... Loop 20
    Day 8 .... Block 22
    Day 9 .... Smash 24
    Day 10 ...... Flip 25
    Day 11 ...... Lob 26
    Day 12 ...... Chop 27
    Day 13 ...... Counterloop 28
    Day 14 ...... The Perfect Strokes 29
    Day 15 ...... The Important Shot 31
    Day 16 ...... The Racket Angle 32

Chapter 3 ...... **Footwork** **34**
    Day 17 ...... The Missing Key in Footwork 35
    Day 18 ...... In-and-Out Footwork 37

Chapter 4 ...... **Serves & Returns** **39**
    Day 19 ...... The Importance of Serving 40
    Day 20 ...... The Details of Perfection 41
    Day 21 ...... Short Fast Serves vs. Short Slow Serves 44
    Day 22 ...... Open Your Eyes   O_O 45
    Day 23 ...... Serving in a New Dimension 47
    Day 24 ...... Varying the Toss 48
    Day 25 ...... Looping Serves 49
    Day 26 ...... Table vs. Your Hand 51
    Day 27 ...... Serving Precision 52

Chapter 5 ...... Game Tactics 54
    Day 28 .... Mandatory Tactics... 55
    Day 29 .... Beat the Looper.. 56
    Day 30 .... Beat the Blocker... 58
    Day 31 .... Beat the Defensive Chopper 59
    Day 32 .... Beat the Attacking Chopper 61
    Day 33 .... Beat the Junk 62
    Day 34 .... Beat the One-Sided Player 64
    Day 35 .... Beat the Wheelchair Player 66
    Day 36 .... Beat the All-Around Player 68
    Day 37 .... Beat the Short-Pips Attacker.............................. 69
    Day 38 .... Beat the Seemiller-Grip Player 70
    Day 39 .... Beat the Traditional Penholder 72
    Day 40 .... Beat the Girl 73
    Day 41 .... Beat the Heavy-Weight Champ 75
    Day 42 .... Beat the Lefty 76
    Day 43 .... Beat Your Friends 78
    Day 44 .... Beat Yourself 79

Chapter 6 ...... Practice 80
    Day 45 .... Effective Practice 81
    Day 46 .... Plan A vs. Plan B.. 83
    Day 47 .... Disappointment... 85
    Day 48 .... Practice Six Days 87
    Day 49 .... What's Next? 88
    Day 50 .... The Attacking Mindset....................................... 90
    Day 51 .... Returning Nets & Edges.................................... 91
    Day 52 .... Slump Busting 93
    Day 53 .... Are You in a Jam?.. 96
    Day 54 .... Trajectories... 98
    Day 55 .... Video Analysis 99
    Day 56 .... Five Ways to Dominate 101

Chapter 7 ...... Tournaments 102
    Day 57 .... Tournament Tough 103
    Day 58 .... Coaching at Tournaments 109
    Day 59 .... Learn What?... 111
    Day 60 .... Jet Lag 113
    Day 61 .... Lucky Loser 114

Day 62 ...... Get Serious in the Morning 115
Day 63 ...... Playing Higher Events 117
Day 64 ...... Scouting 119
Day 65 ...... Statistics 123
Day 66 ...... The Two-Minute Warm-up 125
Day 67 ...... The Checklist 127
Day 68 ...... Kids 129
Day 69 ...... When to Complain 131
Day 70 ...... You Can't Stop Him 133

Chapter 8 ...... Mental Strength.. 134
Day 71 ...... Proper Execution 135
Day 72 ...... Pre-Game Routine 136
Day 73 ...... Post-Game Routine 137
Day 74 ...... Throw a Curve Ball 138
Day 75 ...... Trouble, Trouble, Trouble 139
Day 76 ...... Guess or Not to Guess.................................... 140
Day 77 ...... Conviction 142
Day 78 ...... The World-Class Mindset 144
Day 79 ...... You are a Loser.. 147
Day 80 ...... Dead Time 150
Day 81 ...... Can You Sense the Future?............................ 152
Day 82 ...... Be the Front Runner 154
Day 83 ...... The Mental Timeout 156

Chapter 9 ...... Health.. 158
Day 84 ...... Eat Up the Competition................................. 159
Day 85 ...... Sleep Positioning 160
Day 86 ...... Table Tennis Fuel.. 161
Day 87 ...... Diets 162
Day 88 ...... Table Tennis Breakfast 164

Chapter 10..... Equipment 165
Day 89 ...... Carbon Blades vs. Wood Blades 167
Day 90 ...... Sponge Thickness 168
Day 91 ...... Sponge Hardness/Density.............................. 169
Day 92 ...... Light Blade vs. Heavy Blade 170
Day 93 ...... Large Head vs. Small Head............................ 171
Day 94 ...... Lifetime of the Rubber.................................... 172

Day 95 .... Got Junk? 173
Day 96 .... Your Backup Racket 174

Chapter 11 ..... Your Future 175
Day 97 .... Thinking Ahead 176
Day 98 .... The Guinea Pig 178
Day 99 .... Try Something New 180
Day 100 ..... Steps to Perfection 182

Glossary 186

Personal Notes 196

Other Resources 202

Introduction

By Larry Hodges
USATT Hall of Famer and USATT Certified National Coach

One hundred days . . . if you live to be 82 years old, that's about 30,000 days. All Coach Samson asks is that you take just a few minutes on 1/3 of 1% of those days to learn something new.

One hundred days . . . that's how long it'll take for coach and player Samson Dubina to lead you through these pages, a few minutes each day, with the goal of taking your game to the next level. He leads you through eleven chapters: Beginnings, Strokes, Footwork, Serves & Returns, Game Tactics, Practice, Tournaments, Mental Strength, Health, Equipment, and Your Future. Just reading the chapter titles gives you a pretty good idea of what you'll be doing.

One hundred days . . . it starts with Basic Principles and Writing Out a Game Plan, and then you get to Strokes – which includes Body Position, Serve, Drive, Push, Loop, Block, Smash, Flip, Lob, Chop, Counterloop, The Perfect Strokes, The Important Shot, The Racket Angle – and we're only through Chapter Two!

One hundred days . . . it's a fraction of the time it takes a top coach like Samson to accumulate the knowledge and experience needed to coach at a high level, and it's yours for the price of this book and a few minutes for one hundred days.

One hundred days . . . if FDR could push through most of the New Deal in that time, think what you could do with your table tennis game! It's about the right amount of time needed to learn and ingrain new techniques and begin the road to taking your game to the next level.

I've watched Samson develop from up-and-coming junior to top player to top coach. He's one of the few top coaches who can put his knowledge into words, as he does regularly on his website, www.samsondubina.com. (See News & Articles.) And now much of that knowledge is yours . . . for one hundred days!

Preface

By Author Samson Dubina

During the next 100 days, I want to take you on a table tennis journey where you will enhance your basics, improve your game tactics, become tournament tough, and develop the necessary tools to move up to the next level. Whether you are at home or at the club, I encourage you to pull out this book and read one short section each day. Throughout your training sessions, try to apply what you learned through your three to five minutes of daily reading. After reading each section, your main daily task during the next 100 days will be to apply what you have learned by taking notes, remembering it, practicing it, and continuing to practice it. Best wishes on your journey to success!

Chapter 1: Beginnings

Day 1
Basic Principles of Table Tennis

As you begin your journey to table tennis perfection during the next 100 days, I want to give you some basic principles to follow.

Developing solid strokes starts with moving the right way. Most professional coaches begin teaching footwork from the first or second lesson. By moving into position for each ball, you can avoid reaching and leaning while learning to be consistent in your spin and control. Even at an elite level, most players practice 3-4 hours each day on their footwork. So, even on the days that you focus on your strokes, your spin, or your placement, try to also work on your foundation, your footwork.

Becoming tournament tough starts with thinking the right way. In tournaments, you have less than ten seconds between points. During this "dead" time, you must be able to quickly analyze what you did right or wrong, be able to calm yourself down, be able to strategize for the next point, and be able to go through your pre-point routine. If you can train yourself to think between points, even in practice matches, you can form insightful tactics during the match and coach yourself. Thinking the right way also involves encouraging yourself and avoiding negative thoughts.

Tournament preparation begins with practicing the right way. Most of the drills during a practice session should be geared to help your game. Try to practice the way you actually play – this seems obvious but is not commonly used. For example, if you are a two-winged looper, then don't merely do forehand footwork. Try to do intense footwork using both your backhand and forehand. If you are a good blocker, then do drills mixing offense and defense. If you have a strong loop against backspin, then start most of your drills with a heavy backspin serve, then loop, and then continue the drill. In addition to that, many players focus each session only on their weak points. It is vitally important to practice your strengths. In order to become a complete player, you must have strong strengths that you can win 5-6 easy points a game with.

Building confidence starts with believing the right way. By staying positive and believing in yourself, you can accomplish much. If you are always criticizing your serve, your footwork, or your beer belly, then you won't have the confidence to play your best. You will play 50% better with confidence – regardless if you are winning or losing.

Major improvement begins with losing the right way. You will probably learn more from losing than from winning. If you win a match, you will probably just want to do the same thing the next match without really thinking "why" you won and "what" you did. However, if you lose, you will more likely consider what you did wrong and what you need to improve. After a hard loss, you will likely return to the practice hall with a renewed focus on what you need to change. Instead of being angry about a loss, look at it as a learning experience to fuel your training motivation. Instead of being resistant to a loss, just realize that it is part of the game, and each loss is merely one stepping stone to greatness.

Learning table tennis begins with starting the right way. In addition to reading this book and coaching yourself, you should consider hiring a professional coach to guide you on your journey. The coach will give you the needed tools to reach a high level as well as advice on tournaments, equipment, practice routines, and physical training.

Day 2
Writing Out a Game Plan

You have probably heard the expression, "If you don't know where you are going, any road will take you there." Well, this saying is also true with your table tennis game.

You should have a long-term goal; this requires hard work over an extended period of time. This goal should be one of the means to fuel your energy and motivate you to practice hard during each training session. To make each practice session more effective, it is important to write out an exact game plan. Today, I'm going to ask you many questions about your game. Get a notebook and write out answers to each of the following questions. Once you have answered these questions, it will be easy for you to write detailed strategies on how to progress your game.

During the next year, look to improve one level; this is a great starting point. If your rating is under 1000, then a level is about 300 points. From 1000-2000 rated, a level is about 200 points. From 2000-2600, a level is about 100 points. Over 2600, a level is about 50 points. Your goal should be to improve your game, not your rating. Your USATT rating just gives a starting point to make your goal.

Start out by watching many players who are one level above you and ask yourself the following questions listed below. Once you have answered these questions, you should have a good idea of what your weaknesses are. It is very important to continue practicing your strengths as well as improving your weaknesses.

How are their serves better than mine?
- Do they have more spin?
- Do they have better placement?
- Do they have more spin/placement variation?
- Do they keep the bounce lower?
- Do they disguise the backswing, contact point, and follow through better than I do?

Note: Serving practice is one of the fastest ways to improve. You just need a table and a bucket of balls. Focus on keeping your short serves spinny and low with good variation. Focus on keeping your long serves fast as a surprise with good placement.

How are their serve returns better than mine?
- Are they able to attack the long serves?
- Are they able to control the short serves with a variety of returns – flip, drop, and long push?
- Are they able to adjust to different spins?
- Are they able to keep the ball low enough?

Note: The best way to progress your serve return game is to play against many different opponents by playing at different table tennis clubs and tournaments. Instead of merely trying to touch the ball back onto the table, learn how to stroke the ball onto the table using spin. Your opponent's spin will affect you less and you will be making it more difficult for your opponent on the next ball.

How are their attacks better than mine?
- Are they able to attack with more power?
- Are they able to attack with better placement?
- Are they able to attack more consistently?
- Are they able to attack with both forehand and backhand?
- Are they able to counterattack against an attack?
- Are they able to consistently attack both backspin and topspin?

Note: Most likely, power is not the main problem. The main difference is usually ball placement and consistency. If you attempt ten opening loops in the first game and miss five of them, it's like spotting your opponent five points before the game even begins.

How is their defense better than mine?
- Are they able to return many different loops?
- Are they able to combine both offense and defense?
- Are they able to vary their defense?
- Are they able to adjust to different kinds of attacks coming at them?

Note: Many attackers only focus on attacking. In tournaments, you cannot always attack first. In this case, you will need to learn how to block, chop, or counterloop. If you have no defense at all, you probably won't move to the next level.

How is their footwork better than mine?
- Are they able to make small steps and adjust for every ball?
- Are they able to make long jumps for the wide angled balls?
- Are they able to move forward and adjust for the slow block?
- Are they able to move in-and-out faster for the short ball?

Note: Footwork is one of the main reasons that top players are very consistent. This takes time to develop. If you improve your balance and footwork, you will see long-term benefits.

How are their game patterns?
Are they able to play comfortable game patterns with consistency?
Are they able to win at least four points per game with their patterns?
Are they able to follow-up with a killer shot after completing the pattern?

How are they able to adjust to the playing conditions?
- Are they able to quickly adjust to strange tables, balls, floor, and lighting?
- Do they have a pre-game warm-up and stretching routine?

Note: Most top players will arrive at a tournament venue three days in advance to adjust to the conditions and prepare well. Even if you can't arrive three days early, I suggest that you arrive at least two hours early to do some light jogging, stretching, basic warmup, footwork, points, rest, and then another brief warm-up just prior to your match.

After you have answered these questions, highlight the areas that you feel are keeping you from that level. During each practice session, make the goal of improving two of your biggest weaknesses. Continually review these questions and update your answers based on how your game is progressing.

Remember to also keep practicing your strengths! By keeping your strengths strong and improving your weaknesses, you will be on your way to the next level.

Chapter 2: Strokes

Day 3
Body Position

A building is only as strong as its foundation and your game is founded on your basics. Most basic strokes should be learned within the first year of playing. Throughout your playing career, you will need to continue to revisit your basics to see if there are any flaws hindering your progress. For today, you will be studying the ready position.

When receiving a serve, you should be positioned across the table from your opponent and slightly more to the backhand side. This means that you will likely need to adjust your stance when playing against a left-handed player. After positioning yourself exactly across from your opponent, you should then take a mini-step to your right because your forehand has more reach than your backhand. Without lunging or diving for the ball, you should be able to return any serve with a simple side step or forward step. In your ready position, your feet should be slightly wider than shoulder width apart and your feet turned slightly outward. By turning your feet slightly outward, your lateral side-to-side movement will be faster and it will also allow you to rotate your body better on your forehand attack. Your knees should be bent, and you should be leaning forward at the waist. Staying low will help you to move better as well as get a better view of the serve trajectory. Your racket should be slightly above the table and clearly in front of your body. The more you lean forward, the more the racket will be in front, therefore you will have a better forehand/backhand transition.

When serving, you should be positioned very close to the table. As you contact the ball low to the table, you should move back about one arm length away from the table and slightly move your feet into position right or left in anticipation of the next return.

Serve and serve return are two of the most important aspects to table tennis perfection. Having a good ready position when receiving and being prepared after serving will allow you the best chance of starting the point the right way.

Day 4
Serve

Improving your serve is one of the fastest ways to boost your level. In a future chapter, you will learn several new aspects of serving in great detail. Today, I would like to share some foundational principles of serving. When learning serves, many players try to develop very tricky motions before developing enough spin. If you first learn a moderate-to-heavy spin serve, then next learning variations with side-spin combos and no-spin is quite easy. Focus on having one very good motion; after that you can begin learning several variations to that motion. If you are a beginner, your primary focus should be to serve legally, with good control. As you gain confidence on your basic forehand and backhand serves you should next focus on slicing across or over or under the ball to get friction, called spin. Once you can spin the serve with both forehand and backhand serves, it is then time to work on the advanced variations — controlling the height of your serve, the depth, the precise placement, the type of spin variation, and the degree of spin variation.

Another critical factor when serving is to develop a serve that matches your game style. If you are a more offensive player and want to attack first, then most of the serves that you should be developing should be short, low serves that make it difficult for your opponent to attack. If you are a defensive player, then serving fast, spinny serves will often force mistakes from your opponent. Experiment with various spins and various motions to see what best matches your game.

Day 5
Drive

One of the first strokes that you must learn as a beginner is the basic drive. When both players are using the drive, it is called a counterdrive because you are countering (or returning) your opponent's drive. Start with your racket angled toward the top of the net and drive over the ball with a forward swing. Focus on keeping your angle set and being consistent. The focus on the basic drive is to learn ball control and racket angle control. If your drive continues to go off the end of the table, try to close your angle down and aim more toward the bottom of the net. If your drive continues to go in the net, try to open your angle up and aim more toward the back wall.

As you become more proficient in driving, you should next try to vary the placement. With a practice partner or robot, hit one drive crosscourt then the next drive down the line. You can also vary the speed of the drive. Hit the first drive at 60% power then hit the next drive at 30% power. If you perfect the control, racket angle, placement, and tempo of the drive, it will be easier for you to master the other strokes as well.

Day 6
Push

Most players that you encounter in a tournament will serve backspin. The safest way to return a backspin serve is with a push. The push is a basic backspin stroke where you step forward with your right foot (for righties) while slicing under the ball and imparting backspin on the ball. Your racket should typically be at a 45 degree angle if contacting the ball on the rise. This angle greatly depends on your opponent's spin and your racket type.

Your main goal when pushing should be spin and control. If you don't impart enough spin on the ball, then your opponent's spin will affect you too much and you will probably miss the serve. By lightly brushing under the ball and imparting spin, you will gain control. As your control improves, you next want to focus on depth and placement.

If you allow the ball to rise to the top of the bounce, it will be difficult to control the push while keeping it low. Instead, you should push the ball when it is rising. By contacting the ball early in the trajectory, it will allow you to keep it low, to vary the depth, to use sharp angles, and it will take the time away from your opponent because he has a shorter reaction time. Try to avoid pushing with too much power. A powerful push tends to float up and out and it is typically a very inconsistent shot. Remember to focus on ball control, spin, placement, and depth.

Day 7
Loop

A "loop" in table tennis is a ball with extreme topspin. So any strokes that are near the table or away from the table, against backspin, against topspin, or any other spin are called loops if they have extreme topspin. If your opponent serves topspin, stay back away from the table, start your racket at the height of the ball and loop by leaning forward and brushing over the north pole of the ball. If your opponent serves backspin, then you might need to move closer to the table, start your racket about 12-18" below the ball, and lift the ball up and over the net while brushing the ball with topspin. The amount of lift on the loop against backspin will greatly depend on the amount of spin on your opponent's serve, the height of your opponent's serve, the speed of your opponent's serve, as well as your positioning and spin. The loop against backspin usually takes about 1-2 years to perfect, so be persistent at learning it while still understanding that it does take hundreds of hours of practice to master the spin and timing.

After you have mastered the basic loop against topspin and the basic loop against backspin, there are several advanced variations that you should practice and eventually be able to use in real matches.

Vary the degree of spin. By adding more or less spin to each ball, you will be able to learn to better control the ball and you will make it more difficult for your opponent to comfortably block your loop. If you add the no-spin variation, be careful not to loop with too much speed. The more topspin that you add to your loop, the more control you will have.

Vary your distance from the table, especially when looping topspin. Against blockers who do not block hard, you need to stay quite close to the table in order to loop. Against some counterattacking/smashing players, you need to give yourself more distance from the table in order to loop. Regardless of who you are up against, it is critical that you are able to smoothly move in-and-out from the table. If you have merely been practicing side-to-side footwork, it is time for you to add the in-and-out variations to your practices.

Vary your ball placement. Improving your ball placement is one of the fastest ways to improve your game. Against those players who are comfortable with both backhand and forehand, you should often target the center transition point. Against those opponents who are trying to play full-table forehand or full-table backhand, you need to work the angles in order to make them play with their weak side. When practicing ball placement, try not to be too self-focused on your stroke, but instead be focused more on your opponent – his strengths and his weaknesses.

Vary the type of spin, especially when looping topspin. By adding various amounts of sidespin to the ball, you can make it much more difficult for your opponent to block or counterloop. Practice adding slight amounts of sidespin to your topspin loop. Once you become consistent at that skill, next try to add more sidespin. The more topspin you apply, the more speed that you can add to your loop. If you loop with pure sidespin or sidespin backspin, make sure that you focus on control, not power.

Day 8
Block

When your opponent attacks strongly, you have basically two defensive options – run away from the table or stay close. When you stay close and make contact with the ball, it is called a block. In modern table tennis, blocking is one of the most under-developed skills in junior programs across the US. Most coaches teach attack, footwork, and serve. However, learning to block really helps with ball control and it is one of the necessary stages in learning the exact timing for counterattacking. If you learn to position the body correctly and contact the ball at the preferred timing, then it will be very easy to learn how to counterloop. Here are a few recommendations that I have for learning the proper block.

The most important aspect of blocking is to have a relaxed grip. As you contact the ball on the rise, think about cushioning it and slowing the speed of the ball.

Keep your racket high and in front of your body. If your racket is too close to your torso, then you will easily get jammed for the middle ball.

Watch where your opponent is attacking, move into position, and then block. If you reach or lean for the block, you won't have much control. Footwork is also something that you can practice with a training partner. Ask him to loop one ball to your wide forehand and one ball to your wide backhand. Practice moving into position and looping with good control.

Watch where your opponent's ball is contacting your side of the table. If it hits close to the net, then you will need to move in and press down slightly on the very top of the ball. If it hits closer to the end-line, then you need to press gently on the back/top of the ball.

When adding a little speed to your block, use your body power. Gently lean into the block and apply the pressure with your body movement.

Placement is the key to successful blocking. If you can consistently place the ball well, then your opponent will likely be off-balance.

Once you have mastered the basic block, it is time to add some variation. By adding a slight amount of sidespin or topspin, you can make it even more challenging for your opponent.

By placing your block in a good location, you can create the opportunity to counterattack. You should often block to the backhand or transition point. If your opponent steps around to use his forehand from the backhand side, then you should often block to his wide forehand. Once your opponent is out-of-position and gives a weak ball, then take the opportunity to counterattack.

Day 9
Smash

The smash is the most powerful shot in the game; this is the finishing shot to put your opponent away. Before smashing the ball, give yourself some distance by moving back slightly. Hold your racket high and behind the ball. Step forward as you smash and drive the ball forward and down. There are three main factors that I would also like to mention about the smash.

You must read your opponent's spin properly. All high balls should not be smashed in the same manner. When you see a high topspin ball, step back slightly, start your racket high, and smash forward and down. When you see a high backspin ball, step forward, start your racket lower and the angle more open, while smashing forward and slightly up.

In order to make your smash more consistent, try to add spin to your smash. A smash with some topspin will possibly be 10% slower, but it will usually have about 50% more control. Be consistent in smashing – add topspin!

As with all strokes, placement is a huge part. When your opponent is near the table, smash to his elbow (his transition point). At the transition point, he will need to make a very quick decision to use backhand or forehand. When he is away from the table, smash more often to the wide angles – especially the wide backhand. When your opponent is far from the table, the court becomes wide. In order to cover the wide angle, he will be forced to move 15-20 feet to reach the angle balls. Take advantage of this distance and make him cover the entire court.

Day 10
Flip

The flip is described as a mini-loop over the table. At the beginner level, flips are commonly used to attack short no-spin or topspin serves. At the intermediate to elite level, flips are used to attack any type of serve – backspin, topspin, no-spin, sidespin, corkscrew, or combination spin serve.

When flipping a topspin or no-spin serve, step forward with your right foot (if you are right handed) while leaning over the table; this will put your body closer to the ball so that you can reach it. Next, start your backswing about 12" behind the contact point and spin over the ball while aiming at the top of the net. At the completion of the shot, immediately return to your ready position based on where you placed your flip. Many flips are returned very quickly. If you don't immediately get back, then you will be stuck blocking the ball while leaning over the table.

When flipping a backspin serve, again you will step forward with your right foot while leaning forward over the table. This time you will need to open your angle more, while starting your backswing close to the contact point. Contact the ball slightly under the equator and lift up as you are spinning the ball up and over the net. Note that it is extremely difficult to flip a very heavy backspin serve that bounces low. There will be times that you might be forced to push instead of loop, and that's ok. If you do choose to flip the very heavy backspin serve, you might want to consider flipping from the side of the ball using your backhand flip. By flipping from the side of the ball, you will be hitting more of the axis point, which isn't spinning quite as fast. When dealing with the heavy backspin serve, focus on lifting with spin, not power. As with the other flips, quickly return to the ready position to prepare for the next ball.

Day 11
Lob

When you are away from the table and hitting the ball high into the air near the ceiling, that shot is called a lob. The lob isn't just used during NBA half-time shows, it is often used by professional players during competition to save the rally and continue the point. There are several keys that you need to focus on in order to improve your lob.

The first needed element is footwork. The further away from the table that you play, the more court side-to-side and forward-and-back you need to play. By anticipating based on your placement, by watching your opponent's racket, and by adjusting for the incoming ball, you can be ready to move and return any smash.

The next needed element is control. By allowing the ball time to drop slightly, it will be easier to return the smash because the ball has already lost much of the speed and spin. To return the smash with control, start your racket slightly below the contact point and brush up on the ball with topspin.

The last element is placement. As you are spinning the ball back, you should be aiming deep on your opponent's side of the table. By placing the lob deep on the table, your opponent will be forced to tone down the smash and drive it forward instead of down. If you accidentally lob the ball near the net, your opponent will be able to use the angles as well as generate tremendous downward force, making it extremely difficult for you to return.

There is another shot similar to lobbing, it is called "fishing." When fishing, you are still away from the table but now returning the ball much lower. The goal with fishing is to eventually work into a counterlooping rally where you can take the attack back.

Day 12
Chop

The chop is quite similar to the push but is used when you are away from the table. By starting your racket high and behind the ball, you then swing down the back of the ball, imparting backspin. Because you are further from the table, your stroke needs to be much longer. The chop can be performed against any spin.

If you are chopping with heavy backspin, then your swing will need to be more back to forward with an open racket. As you chop, try to aim fairly high above the net because the backspin will dig the ball down as it contacts your racket.

If you are chopping with light backspin, no-spin, or sidespin ball, then your swing can be slightly down as you brush under the ball. Keep in mind that it is more difficult to spin a no-spin ball than a ball that is already spinning. If you don't put good focus on brushing the no-spin ball, you won't have much control and you will be producing a "wobbling" chop.

If you are chopping against a loop with heavy topspin, then you need to be much further from the table. Start your racket high above the ball and chop down toward the floor as you also move your body down slightly. Keep your angle more closed and aim low. The ball will tend to pop up. Reading the spin and speed of the incoming loop and timing it appropriately are the keys to chopping against a loop with a lot of topspin.

Unless you are a defensive player, learning how to chop isn't that beneficial. If you are a beginner, I recommend that you focus on other areas of the game first. If you are an advanced player, then you can consider learning the chop as a change of pace during a long rally when you are away from the table.

Day 13
Counterloop

When an opponent loops the ball at you, your first reaction might be to go into a defensive position for blocking or chopping. For the beginner, this is the most consistent plan. If you are an advanced looper, then I would recommend that you learn how to loop his loop back to him; this shot is called the counterloop. There are a few key elements that you need to focus on when counterlooping.

First, find your preferred distance. Some players like to counterloop from close to the table using a very short swing, while other players step back from the table, allowing the ball to drop and using a longer swing. Once you find your distance and your feet are set, it is much easier to counterloop.

Next, keep your center of gravity low by bending your knees and leaning forward. Take a short backswing and contact the ball in front of your body. If you contact the ball beside or behind you, then your loop will likely go too long. The key is to hit in front of your body in order to drive the loop forward and keep it low.

Finally, play it safe with placement. As you become more proficient in counterlooping, it will then be time to go for excellent placement. However, for the beginning to intermediate player, it is okay to counterloop crosscourt. It is extremely difficult to land a counterloop down the line or at a very sharp angle. For now, here are the key elements to focus on: ball control, positioning, balance, contact point, and spin.

Day 14
The Perfect Strokes

During tournaments, you have probably heard many players commenting about various strokes...
"He has good strokes!"
"His strokes are wrong!"
"How is he rated over 2000 with strokes like that?"
"His loop is very smooth!"
"He won the tournament, but he doesn't have the best strokes."
"His strokes are old-school!"
"Wow, his strokes flow nicely together!"

There are always many comments flying around tournaments regarding strokes. So, how do you know if your strokes are good or not? Is it personal opinion? Is it what your friends tell you? Is it defined as what the top players are currently using? In the past few days, we have talked about several types of strokes. Today, I would like for you to step back and consider your own strokes that you currently have.

Good strokes all have several common elements. If all of these elements are true about your strokes, then you probably are on your way to success. If these elements are not true about your strokes, then you need to make some changes.

#1: With good strokes, you should be able to easily change the location on your shot. For example, if your forehand flip is good, then you should be able to easily flip to the wide backhand, middle, and wide forehand. If you cannot hit all those locations, then you need to make a change to your backswing, body positioning, or wrist positioning.

#2: With good strokes, you should be able to impart various speeds and spins on the ball. For example, if you have a very good sidespin serve, then you should be able to easily vary it with long and short variations as well as side-backspin and side-topspin variations. If you can only impart one degree of speed and spin, then your opponent can easily adjust to your game as the match progresses. With good speed and spin changes on all of your strokes, you can keep your opponent off-balance. Elite players can smoothly change gears on their strokes, and that should be your personal goal as well.

#3: With good strokes, you should be able to adjust the height and length of your backswing, and your follow-through based on the speed, spin, and trajectory of the incoming ball. For example, you must have a great backhand loop that works well against a consistent block BUT ALSO a great backhand loop that works against long serves, heavy pushes, fast blocks, and dead blocks. If you cannot adjust your technique, then having a backhand loop will not be very beneficial in tournaments.

#4: With good strokes, you should be able to play without serious injuries. Many table tennis injuries are due to poor technique. For example, if you are using only arm on your forehand, then you will likely have shoulder injuries over time. When an injury arises, ask yourself if it is possibly due to bad technique. Relaxed strokes rarely lead to extreme injuries; whereas stiff muscles develop muscle soreness and injury.

If you have major changes that need to be made, then it is essential to buy a camcorder and watch your practice sessions and matches. Compare your strokes to the professional players' strokes and make the needed changes. Once you have made the full evaluation, be willing to return again and again to the camcorder throughout your practice sessions to make sure that you are maintaining the correct stroke during the warm-up, footwork drills, multiball drills, robot drills, and games.

Day 15
The Important Shot

You might think that if you win a spectacular rally or win an easy point, it just counts as one point. But, actually, you might be wrong.

Let me give you a scenario. You are winning 9-7 in the final game. You serve short topspin and your opponent reads your serve as backspin. He steps forward and pushes your short topspin serve giving you an incredibly easy popup. At point-blank range, it would have been nearly impossible for him to return your powerful weapon, BUT unfortunately for you ... you miss your smash!

The score should have been 10-7, with you being very pumped and excited. Because you missed your powerful smash, the score is now 9-8 with you being depressed and your opponent feeling new hope. When you miss a winning shot, there is a two-point swing. You could have won a point. But instead, your opponent won a point. Also there is often a mental swing which usually affects the game by 1-2 points. So, when you missed the easy smash at 9-7, *it likely costs you three points total!*

Here are some additional points to ponder:
1. Remember that each hit is important – there are no easy ones.
2. Remember that you must be fully focused when smashing, move into position, adjust your swing based on the height and speed and spin and bounce, while accelerating through the point of contact and adding some topspin to your smash.

Remember that returning a smash from your opponent will have the same effect – a two-point swing in the game plus a mental advantage.

Day 16
The Racket Angle

During my years of coaching, the #1 question that players ask me is in regard to the correct racket angle when looping. Having the correct racket angle for each particular stroke is important. However, there are many, many, many factors that need to be calculated within a split second to adjust your racket angle to properly loop the ball.

1. The height of the incoming ball
2. The depth of the incoming ball
3. The speed of the incoming ball
4. The type and amount of spin on the incoming ball
5. The trajectory of the incoming ball
6. Your body position
7. Your racket height
8. Your backswing
9. The amount of tension in your arm
10. Your racket speed

11. The desired height of your loop
12. The desired depth of your loop
13. The desired speed of your loop
14. The desired amount and type of spin on your loop
15. The desired trajectory of your loop
16. The type of rubber that you are using (inverted, pips, etc.)
17. The amount of grip on the rubber you are using (slick, somewhat grippy, or tacky)

To make 17 calculations and adjust your racket angle within a matter of ½ second take a lot of practice. No wonder the top players practice 6-8 hour per day for years and years to reach a high level. At this point in your game, you can focus somewhat on adjusting your racket angle. However, your primary focus should be on the other aspects that we talked about this week such as body positioning, backswing, contact point, follow through, and maintaining good spin on each shot. If you have those aspects mastered along with good spin, then having the exact angle isn't quite as much of a critical factor.

Chapter 3: Footwork

Day 17
The Missing Key in Footwork

So how good is your footwork? Most club players are unable to excel in table tennis because of their poor footwork. Many players blame their beer belly or their age or their footwear or their training partners. However, the aspect of footwork that I will be describing in this short article is an aspect that every player can improve upon, regardless of their age, rating, or physical condition. Today, I want to show you the importance of anticipation as it relates to footwork in table tennis. There are three elements that I want you to remember.

First, move into position based on your shot. If you are positioned at your forehand corner and you hit crosscourt, you are probably in a good position for the next shot. If your opponent decides to hit down-the-line, then you can adjust your position. But covering the crosscourt ball will force your opponent to hit the more difficult down-the-line ball or to hit the easy ball to your position. From your forehand corner you hit to the middle, you then need to move to the middle of the table. From your forehand corner you hit down-the-line to your opponent's backhand, you then need to shift your feet to the backhand corner in anticipation of the next ball. Again, there is no guarantee that the ball will go crosscourt. The only thing that you are trying to accomplish in this first element is that you cover the easiest and deadliest shot from your opponent – crosscourt.

In order to practice this first aspect, I would recommend starting simple and perfecting the first ball first. Start by serving to the corners and preparing with your body position for the cross court return. You can do the same with serve return. Have your training partner serve short backspin, you push deep to either corner, then prepare cross court to block his loop.

Second, adjust your position again based on what you see. If you have moved into position on the backhand side of the table but you see your opponent's racket angled toward the middle, then re-adjust your position based on what you see. About 90% of the time, the angle is correct. Players usually don't double-fake you. If your opponent's angle is showing that he is hitting to your forehand, then usually your opponent is truly hitting to your forehand.

In order to practice this second aspect, I would recommend learning how to watch the ball as it approaches you, then learning how to watch your opponent's racket after your hit. Warm up forehand to forehand with your training partner. Ask your training partner to occasionally switch to your backhand. You should be able to see his angle change prior to contact. If you can see the angle change and are able to adjust, then you are on the right track. If your training partner hits the ball to your backhand ... the ball is crossing the net ... then suddenly you realize that he switched, you have not properly been watching his angle. Start with simple drills like this, then get more advanced as you perfect this new skill.

Third, be ready to make small, split-second adjustments with your feet. The anticipation based on your shot and the anticipation based on your opponent's angle are very general. You might think that your opponent is placing the ball to your middle-forehand, but in fact, he placed the ball to your wide forehand. In order to maintain balance and control, you must make the final adjustment with your feet.

In order to practice this third aspect, ask your training partner to block for you in the forehand ½ table. You hit everything to his forehand while he moves you slightly. Your feet should be making 1-2 micro moves before every hit. The world's best players usually take about 2-3 mini-steps between hits.

Remember the three aspects – your shot, your opponent's racket, and your final adjustment. If you can master these three aspects, then table tennis will seem easier, you will seem to have more time, you will be reading the ball better, and the game will flow much easier.

Day 18
In-And-Out Footwork

About 99% of the time, players practice side-to-side footwork moving from forehand to backhand and backhand to forehand. I rarely see players practice in-and-out footwork, but in fact ... these players are missing a key element of the game. Today, I'm going to outline 10 situations where in-and-out footwork is absolutely necessary.

1. You must learn to move in when your opponent chops the ball. For example, you are eight feet away from the table in a counterlooping rally against a chopper and he surprises you with a chop. You must move in to properly loop the ball.
2. You must learn to move in when your opponent mixes in an anti-block. For example, you are playing against a Seemiller grip player and he is blocking fast to the corners. Suddenly, he flips his racket to anti and gives a dead block, you must move in to properly loop the ball.
3. You must learn to move in when your opponent has a miss-hit. For example, you are in an intense rally away from the table and

your opponent swings hard but the ball hit the edge of his racket. If the ball bounces short, you must move in to properly loop the ball.
4. You must learn to move in when your opponent hits the net. For example, during the rally you are expecting a deep ball, but your opponent's ball hits the net and barely drops over on your side. The ball is so short that it would be nearly impossible to reach it. You must move in to properly return the net ball.
5. You must learn to move back slightly after your serve. For example, you serve short backspin and your opponent pushes deep to your backhand. It is very difficult to backhand loop against backspin when you are pinned against the table. You must move back in order to properly loop the ball.
6. You must learn to move back after receiving a short serve. For example, your opponent serves very, very short and you receive the serve with a short push. Next, you must prepare back for the flip or deep push.
7. You must learn to move back after receiving a half-long serve. For example, your opponent serves a serve that just barely comes long enough to loop. You move forward and loop the ball with your forehand to your opponent's forehand. You must move back slightly in order to properly prepare for the incoming block or counterloop.
8. You must learn to move back slightly against a power-blocker. For example, you loop a backspin ball and your opponent jams a fast block. If you stay too close to the table, you will likely be forced to block his block, which is a weak shot. You must move back slightly in order to continue looping his fast blocks.
9. You must learn to move back slightly when counterlooping. Sometimes you can counterloop from near the table. Other times, it is necessary to give yourself enough distance, lean forward, and counterloop with speed and spin away from the table.
10. You must learn to move back when a sudden lob surprises you. For example, you are in a topspin rally from near the table, your opponent surprises you with a deep, heavy topspin lob that hits near your end-line. By backing up slightly, you can lean forward and contact the ball on the top of the bounce, giving excellent power.

Chapter 4:
Serve and Serve Return

Day 19
The Importance of Serving

Many players neglect to practice their serves on a regular basis and really miss out on a vital aspect of improvement. Today, I would like to share four general reasons that serves are so important. In future days, I'll be detailing how to improve your serves.

Reason #1: Every point starts with a serve and serve return. If you have a high-level serve, that is one weapon that your opponent can't take away from you! If you start the point with an advantage, then hopefully you can continue to dominate throughout the rest of the point.

Reason #2: By serving low, short, and with good variation in spin and placement, you should be able to attack first. When two attacking players are competing, whoever attacks first often wins the point. So, your serve sets up your attack!

Reason #3: If you have a strong serve, you can somewhat anticipate what is coming next. A fast serve to the backhand will likely be returned with a deep return. A short, very heavy backspin serve will often be returned with a push. A short, heavy topspin serve will often be returned with a flip.

Reason #4: By having a tricky serve that wins many points in a match, you will have an advantage mentally. Nothing is more traumatizing to your opponent than to have a serve that he just can't seem to return!

Even though you might find it boring, practicing your serves regularly will pay off!

Day 20
The Details of Perfection

Improving your serve is one of the fastest ways to progress your game. Today, you will learn ten ways to improve your serve:

1. Use the serves that best set up your game
2. Train them in a tournament environment
3. Miss some serves
4. Use your best serves early
5. Vary the quality of spin
6. Remember to attack
7. Be willing to sacrifice a couple points
8. Train them to perfection
9. Use visualization
10. Play practice matches

Let's look at these one by one.
1. The most important aspect to serving is to use the serves that most effectively set up your game. Even if you can't win the point with an "ace," at least you can set up the point to play the style you want to play. Take the time now to outline a detailed game-plan so that you can have a clear understanding of your style and the strengths in your game. If you are a looper, then most of your serves should be short, low backspin. If you are a pips-out attacker, you should serve mostly fast long with good placement. If you are a chopper, then you should serve deep spinny serves. Once you have determined which serves best set up your game, develop a motion in which you can serve either short or long with the same motion and at least two different spins with the same motion.

2. When practicing your serves, do them in a tournament environment. First, try to be tired when you serve. Do jumping jacks or footwork so that your hand will be sweaty and it will be challenging to concentrate. Second, practice in tournament conditions. Try to use a tournament table and 3-star balls so that the bounce will be similar to what you will be using in the tournament. If you are trying to serve short, the ball will probably go slightly longer in a tournament. For this reason, I suggest covering the last three inches on the opponent's side of the table when you serve. This will force you to serve slightly shorter during practice. Third, when doing serve practice, think of specific opponents. What serves have worked well against this opponent previously? How would this particular opponent receive this serve? Fourth, use these same serves at the club. Don't save your serves for a tournament – be willing to use them in practice matches.

3. In practice, you should try to put so much spin on the ball that you miss about 10-20% of your serves. In tournaments, you should try to put so much spin on the ball that you miss about 2% of your serves. If you are not missing any serves, that is an indication that you are not trying hard enough. In tournaments, you should usually miss about one serve per match. If you miss too many serves, you will be hurting yourself.

4. By serving your best serves early, you can build an initial lead in the match and gain confidence. I recently beat an opponent who had a very tricky serve. In three games, I only returned one out of seven of these particular tricky serves. However, I won the match 3-0 in games. Once the serve started working, he should have continued using it. He wanted to save it for "a closer", which never came because he lost 3-0 in games.

5. As I mentioned in the above paragraph, if a serve is working, keep using it! If you change your serve too often, you might confuse yourself. Instead of jumping from one serve to another, sometimes use the same serve with the same spin, but vary the placement and quality of spin.

6. Remember to attack. Your serve will seem ten times more threatening if it is backed by a vicious attack. If your opponent is trying to keep you from attacking, he will make many mistakes trying to keep the ball short and low. Personally, my serves work the best when my attacking game is at its best.

7. During the game, be willing to sacrifice a couple of points. Many players are afraid to serve long against a looper, so they always serve short. This allows the looper to stay closer to the table when returning serve and be prepared for the short serve. Sometimes you must serve fast down-the-line or to the backhand or to the middle just to keep the opponent guessing. You might lose a single point, but all your short serves will be much more effective later when your opponent must give you some respect for your long serve.

8. When practicing serves, train them to perfection. Focus for 30 minutes on one particular serve. Take your time and analyze it serve by serve—what you did right and what you did wrong. Study how the world's top players serve that particular serve, by watching their backswing, body movement, contact point, racket angle, follow through, and ball positioning.

9. Regardless if you are practicing in the basement, playing at the club, or competing in a tournament, it is vitally important to visualize your serve and the possible returns prior to serving. Visualize your stance, your toss, your contact point, the ball's contact on your side, the trajectory, and the contact on your opponent's side. Visualize the common returns and your responses while also being prepared to adjust for unpredictable returns.

10. The final link to professional serves is to use them in actual games. Trying to hide secret serves and never using them will not develop your serves to their fullest potential. Use them in practice matches and use them in tournaments. Improving your serve is the fastest way to progress your game. Use the ten techniques listed above and you will be seeing excellent results within a few weeks!

Day 21
Short Fast Serves vs. Short Slow Serves

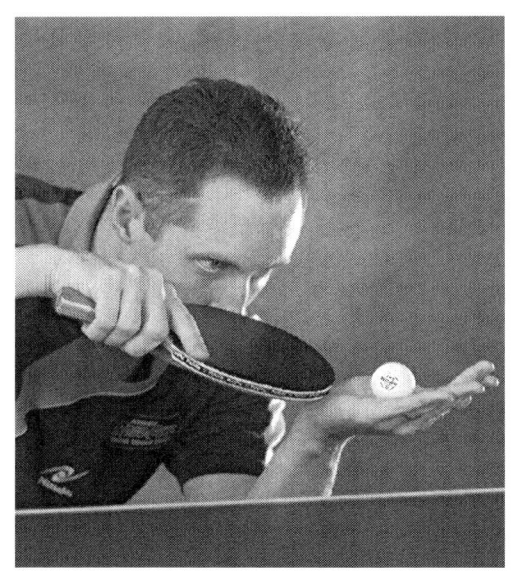

Most club players have two types of serves – long ones and short ones. Today, I'm going to talk about two different types of short serves – fast short serves and slow short serves.

A fast short serve is impacted very close to the server's end-line, travels over the net and quickly hits twice on the receiver's side. This serve is very difficult for the receiver, because he needs to quickly decide if it is long or short. The answer – it is usually half long.

A slow short serve is lofted from the racket very close to the net, travels over the net slowly and usually hits at least 3-4 times on the receiver's side. This serve is much easier to keep short, but it can be slightly more difficult to keep low.

It is good to use a blend of both types. When playing tournaments, I recommend that you often serve the slow one first. Although your opponent might receive it fairly easily, the variation gives them trouble. Next, you should serve the fast short serve. Your opponent will often take a big backswing seeing the ball coming faster, then he will be surprised when the serve also double bounces.

Against opponents who want to flip your serve, I recommend that you often serve the fast short serve while keeping it low and fairly deep while still maintaining two bounces on your opponent's side.

Against opponents who want to loop your medium-long serve, you should often serve the short slow serve while keeping it very short to make sure they can't loop first.

Day 22
Open Your Eyes O_O

Winning tournaments isn't merely about having fast footwork and a powerful loop. Winning is often determined by how poorly you can make your opponent play. In many other sports like swimming or running or weight lifting, you compete and your opponent competes. Your job in running is to perform well yourself. However, your job in table tennis is to hinder your opponent. I'm going to be very blunt here ... If your opponent doesn't miss, then you can't score a single point! Think about that for a minute...

With that said, your primary concern in table tennis should be ... how can I mess up my opponent?! There are literally thousands of ways to take him out of his comfort zone, but today I'm going to talk about one way – serving. How can you take him out of his comfort zone with your serve? Each opponent has a preferred way that he likes to return serves; he might prefer to backhand flip or forehand loop or backhand push or drop shot. Before serving, look at your opponent and ask yourself the question, "How does my opponent want to receive my serve?"

So how do you know how your opponent wants to receive the serve? Can you read his mind? No, but you can read his body language and you can remember how he previously received other serves. In order to read his body, look out of the corner of your eye…

- If he is too close to the table, then a deep, fast, heavy backspin serve to the body will likely force him to push back long.

- If he is too far from the table, then it will be difficult for him to drop shot on a short serve because the momentum from his forward movement will push the ball long.

- If he is waiting for a forehand loop by standing significantly too far to the backhand side, then the short and wide forehand is usually open.

- If he is preparing to do his backhand banana flip over the table, then a deep serve to the backhand will be difficult for him to return.

The possibilities are endless. If you develop the habit of glancing at your opponent and asking yourself the right questions, then you will be well on your way to making him play your game instead of letting him play his game.

Day 23
Serving in a New Dimension

Throughout the last 20 years, when returning serves, most of the world's best players have looped the long serves and pushed short on the short serves. In order to attack first, about 90% of the elite serves have been short. This information has trickled down to even the lowest of the club level players. I heard many, many, many club players repeating, "C'mon, serve short!" SERVING SHORT has been a theme of coaches and players in an attempt to stop the receiver from looping the serve.

SPIN has also been a major theme. Serving with spin often tricks the opponent and gives several free points each game.

HOWEVER, the new theme is LOW! After Zhang Jike won the 2011 world championships, 2012 Olympics, and 2013 World Championships, many young aspiring American players have put a strong emphasis on flipping the serve. With the new emphasis on flipping, the critical serving element is the height of the serve. By keeping your serve with a low trajectory, you will be able to accomplish one of two reasonable possibilities…

First Possibility: Your opponent won't be able to flip your serve. If he pushes, this allows you to attack more easily.

Second Possibility: Your opponent won't be able to flip your serve very hard. If he flips fairly soft, you should be able to easily loop his flip.

It is great to have a short spinny serve, but the top priority should be the height of the serve. Contact the ball as low as possible, and slightly drop your body down about 1" as you contact the ball. Make sure the entire trajectory remains low and that your first bounce on the opponent's side is less than 4" high. If your opponent is unable to flip your serve or unable to flip your serve hard, then you are on the right track! Serve short, serve spinny, and remember to serve LOW!

Day 24
Varying the Toss

When serving, you likely think about the spin, speed, trajectory, and placement. Do you ever consider the height of your toss? Obviously, the ball needs to be projected up a minimum of six inches, but there is no maximum height at which the ball can be tossed.

After presenting the ball to serve and throwing it up, your opponent will need to wait for 0.5-3 seconds before hitting the ball. If you vary your toss, his mind might not be fully ready. For example, your first three serves might be short backspin serves using a high toss of 10-12' in the air. It takes about 2-3 seconds for a serve that high to be projected up, come down, and travel across the net. After a few serves, the receiver is thinking that he has a couple seconds to prepare. Suddenly, on your fourth serve, you give a 6" toss and serve fast down-the-line to his wide forehand. His muscles might not be ready to make the quick movement because his body thought that he had two more seconds to wait.

Varying the toss is one of the unique variations that you can add to possibly win a few extra points each match and keep your opponent feeling uncomfortable.

Day 25
Looping Serves

Looping serves is a bit more challenging than many players imagine. However, if you follow the right thought process and use the right technique, then you will be on your way to major improvement. Here are some steps…

1. Watch the opponent's positioning at the table and body language to possibly see if he will serve short or long.

2. Next, watch his backswing, contact point, and where the ball contacts his side of the table. At this point, you need to start adjusting your feet while keeping your hand in front.

3. Next, watch as the ball contacts your side of the table. If it hits in the first half (near the net), then it will likely be short and you need to adjust in with your legs, upper body, and racket. If it hits in the back half of the table, then it will likely be long enough to loop. These balls will vary based on spin as well.

4. Next, if the serve is half-long, then prepare to loop by keeping your knees bent, adjusting near the table with your body, and shortening your backswing while starting at the appropriate height and angle. If it is heavy backspin, then start lower and open your angle. If it is no-spin, then start higher and close your angle slightly. If the serve is fast and long, then give yourself plenty of space from the table, start at the appropriate height, let the ball come back, then spin the ball.

5. Next, focus on spinning the ball with good placement. The more spin that you are able to create when looping this serve, the easier it will be to control the ball. Without applying enough spin, your opponent's spin will bite into your rubber and cause more errors. Generally, you should loop the half-long balls with about 30-60% power and you should loop the deep serves with about 50-80% power.

Common Pitfalls
1. Neglecting to watch your opponent's racket!
2. Neglecting to move your feet based on the opponent's racket angle and incoming ball!
3. Neglecting to adjust your racket starting position based on the opponent's spin!
4. Neglecting to make a secondary adjustment with your feet!
5. Neglecting to apply enough spin to the ball!

Day 26
Table vs. Your Hand

The score was 9-9 in the final game, your opponent served a half-long serve to your backhand, and you thought that the serve was long enough to loop, but it wasn't. With a full backswing, you looped right into the table! Ouch! As blood began to gush from the back of your hand, you wondered to yourself how this could have been prevented. Today, I'm going to give you ten tips on how to make peace with the edge of the table.

1. Move both feet properly into position.
2. Keep your hand in front of your body and slightly above the table so that you can properly decide whether to push, loop, or flip.
3. Read the bounce on your side to see if the first bounce is deep toward your end-line or short near the net.
4. Take a short backswing when looping the half-long ball.
5. Swing over the table if the serve is topspin, sidespin, or no spin, making sure your strongest acceleration is after you have passed the edge realizing that the table will not come up and bite you.
6. Allow the ball to come off the end of the table if it is backspin.
7. Take a very controlled swing when pushing the half-long ball, focusing on spin and placement rather than speed.
8. Keep a relaxed grip on the racket in case you decide to change your mind at the last second.
9. Step back after looping to properly prepare for the rally.
10. Look to follow-up strong on the next ball.

Many serves go long enough to loop. Looking to loop those serves is the most neglected aspect of looping half-long serves. Expect half-long serves, look for half-long serves, and try to loop half-long serves during each practice session, club match, and tournament. Also, realize that it is merely the first step in the process of winning the point. Expect the rally to continue and always be thinking about the next ball; and continually think to yourself "what is coming next ... what is coming next ... what is coming next..."

Day 27
Serving Precision

When serving, many players focus on height, deception, speed, spin, and placement. These elements are very important. However, the main reason that you need to practice serving is to develop precision. If you have control over all aspects of your serve, it is easy to control the rally when you are serving. Here are a few consequences of having poor precision…

A. You accidentally served long (when trying to serve short) and Ma Long rips the ball for a winner. With more precision, you would have been able to better control the depth of your serve. This is a very common mistake. You were expecting a push from your short serve, but you were punished by a surprise loop because you weren't able to control your serve with proper precision.
B. You accidentally served short to the middle (when trying to serve to the short forehand) and Zhang Jike steps in for an easy backhand flip. With more precision, you would have been able to better control the placement to the forehand making it more difficult for him to use his powerful backhand flip.

C. You accidentally served long to the forehand (when trying to serve long to the elbow) and Wang Hao loops with extreme power wide to your forehand for a winner. With more precision, you would have been able to better control the placement making it more difficult for him to smoothly loop with his forehand. By serving long to the elbow, Wang Hao would have had to make a quick decision to use his forehand or backhand and would likely have given a weaker return.
D. You accidentally served short and high no-spin (when trying to serve low heavy backspin) and Ma Lin finishes you off with a flip-kill. With more precision, you would have been able to serve with more backspin, forcing him to push or give a weaker flip.

In order to master this skill of precision and control on your serve, you should be practicing your serves at least twice per week. A good, tricky serve is only effective if you have control over it and can serve with the intended spin, speed, variation, height, depth, and placement. If you have precision when serving, you can somewhat predict what type of ball is probably coming next. When you can predict what is coming, then it is much easier to form a game plan for the next several balls.

Chapter 5: Game Tactics

Day 28
Mandatory Tactics

When playing a tournament, you might not be familiar with your opponent. Today, I am going to list a few quick things to look for in the first 30 seconds of a match. Implement these ideas, and you will immediately find tactics for the upcoming match.

1. Rubber: Before the match begins, shake hands with your opponent and ask if you can see his racket. Using the ball, very gently check the rubber's friction; the more friction that top-sheet has, the more spin your opponent will be able to impart. Be sure to check both sides because your opponent might have a combination racket with two different kinds of rubber. You should also check the bounce, which is particularly important if your opponent has pips or anti-spin rubber.
2. Grip: When your opponent is holding his racket in the ready position, see if he is using a forehand grip or a backhand grip. A forehand grip has the top of the racket shifted slightly to the thumb side of the hand. A backhand grip has the racket shifted slightly to the index finger side of the hand.
3. Stance: Before serving, check to see if your opponent is standing with his feet parallel to the table (backhand stance) or with his right foot back (forehand stance for righties).
4. Aggressiveness: After the first two points, stop and think to yourself, "Is my opponent offensive or defensive?" If he is winning most of his points attacking, then you must find ways to stop his powerful weapons. If he is winning most of his points by long rallies and allowing you to make mistakes, then you need to be patient, eliminate unnecessary errors, and choose the right ball.

Implementing these four quick tips will allow you to begin making a game-plan to beat your opponent. As the match progresses, be willing to change your original plan.

Day 29
Beat the Looper

    In order to beat a looper, you must first understand his game plan. Then you will have a clear understanding as to what you should do against him. A looper is a player who wants to attack with strong topspin strokes. He could be a forehand looper, backhand looper, or a two-wing looper who attacks with both forehand and backhand. He usually starts with short serves and looks for a long push so that he can start looping. When the looper is on offense, he continues to loop until the point is finished. When the looper is on defense, he usually blocks with his backhand and counterloops with his forehand.

So what do you need to do? Force your game on him and take his weapons away. Since he is a looper, he probably wants to loop. You need to find a way to force him into a defensive position because chopping, blocking, and lobbing probably aren't his strengths. You should serve short most of the time and attempt to attack first, thus forcing the looper into defense. If you loop soft, don't loop to his strong forehand (he will probably be comfortable counterlooping this ball for a winner). Usually your opening loop should be to his weaker counterattacking side—ordinarily middle or backhand. After the start of the rally, surprise him with a strong shot, sometimes even to the wide forehand. After he moves back to retrieve that ball with his wide forehand, attack his wide backhand in order to force him into a defensive position because he probably can't consistently backhand counterloop from off the table.

Key Points
1. Serve short
2. Return short
3. Attack first as much as possible
4. Initially attack his middle or backhand
5. Play against his weaker side more often
6. Give some surprises to the wide forehand
7. If counterlooping away from the table, change to his backhand side as soon as possible

Day 30
Beat the Blocker

If you learn to think what your opponent is thinking, it will be easier for you to understand how you should be playing against him. Today, you will learn how to beat a blocker. What does he want to do? He likely plays with consistency and placement, borrowing your power and returning the ball with quick angles. His goal is to counter your every move and keep the ball in play until you miss. Keep in mind that some blockers are more aggressive than others, so your tactics are going to vary slightly based on the exact style of blocker that you are up against. In this next paragraph, you will learn how to play against the defensive blocker who doesn't attack much.

So what do you need to do against this passive yet very consistent opponent? Serve deep, push deep, loop deep! Hitting the ball with good variation in the last nine to twelve inches of the table will eliminate the sharp angles and force him onto his heels. Don't worry about forcing the attack first. His opening attack and footwork probably aren't very strong; you should be able to counterattack easily. Look for a weak side. He will have one preferred side, either forehand or backhand; and you should be able to identify this within the first several points. With slow footwork, the blocker will have difficulty hiding his weak side. Also, before you begin the match, check for a combination racket; there is a high probability that the blocker is using an unconventional rubber (long pips or anti).

Key Points
1. Serve deep to eliminate the angles
2. Push deep to get a long return
3. Loop deep in the last four inches
4. Check for combination racket
5. Identify his weak side
6. Counterattack against his weak opening

Day 31
Beat the Defensive Chopper

When playing against the defensive chopper, be aware of the fact that he wants to extend the rallies and win points from your mistakes. He will often serve long (hoping that you will attack) and give low, deep pushes. If you loop, he will go away from the table and give spinny chops. He moves well side-to-side and covers the wide balls fairly easily. Instead of winning points with strong attacks, he is waiting for your errors.

So what should you do? You should be patient and selective in choosing the right ball. If the first ball is low, control it with a good push or controlled loop. Be selective on when to attack. Often attack to his middle (the transition point), forcing him to make a decision between backhand and forehand. Move the chopper in-and-out from the table until he gives a high chop that you can finish for a winner. Be aware that if he pushes your push with inverted, it will likely be fairly heavy. If he pushes with pips, the ball will have much less spin or could possibly be no-spin or light topspin; this greatly depends on the amount of spin you imparted and the type of rubber that the chopper is using. If he chops your loop with the pips, his chop will probably be heavy, but proportional to the spin that you loop. If you loop with lots of spin, the pips chop will be heavier; if you loop with less spin, the pips chop will be lighter. If the chopper chops your loop with inverted, it could have a variety of spins, but will likely be light or medium backspin. You should usually focus on pushing to the pips (to get an easier push) and focus on looping to the inverted (to get a lighter chop). Against this chopper, keep the game fairly simple. Because he doesn't attack, you can keep your pushes slightly higher and your loops slightly higher to ensure consistency throughout the entire rally.

Key Points
1. Be consistent and patient until the right ball comes
2. Use safe loops and pushes until the opportunity arises
3. Attack strong when the opportunity arises
4. Keep it simple—loop one, push one
5. Placement to the playing elbow
6. Move him in-and-out
7. Push to the pips
8. Loop to the inverted
9. Take your time between points and remain calm

Day 32
Beat the Attacking Chopper

Be careful! Unlike yesterday's defensive player, this chopper uses his defense to set up his very strong offense. He will try to attack first; but if you attack, he will be consistent while waiting for his opportunity. He loops well with the forehand on the deep ball and attacks well with the backhand on the short ball. After serving deep, he is looking for a good ball to attack with his strong forehand. If you attack first, he will go back and chop, while waiting to counterattack. If you push, then he will move forward and attack with his quick backhand or forehand.

So what should you do? Against this chopper, it is critical that you attack first. If you are forced to push or block, focus on placing the ball well. Even if you can't stop his attack, at least you can place the ball in a position that he can't attack strong. Serve mainly short anywhere or deep to his backhand. When attacking, try to attack mainly to the middle or backhand. When pushing, push to the short forehand or deep backhand.

Key Points
1. Serve short anywhere or long to the backhand
2. Try to attack first
3. Attack strong when the opportunity arises
4. Loop mainly to the backhand or middle
5. When defending, remember to keep the ball low and well placed
6. When pushing, push to the short forehand or deep backhand

Day 33
Beat the Junk

Your opponent who uses long pips or anti-spin rubber wants you to use YOUR OWN SPIN to confuse you. Anti and long pips don't create their own spin. This player is hoping that you will juice up your heavy sidespin serves then keep looping with heavy topspin 'til you drop. He is just going to keep the ball in play and move you around.

So what do you need to do? KISS—keep it simple, sweetheart. Serve deep and fast, no spin or very light spin. This way, it will be simple to attack a high dead ball that isn't angled sharply to the side. Seems easy ... well it is. Because anti and long pips don't have a deep trajectory, the unconventional rubber player will have trouble playing deep and low from your long serve. In order to clear the net, the long pips/anti serve return must be slightly higher. His anti/pips racket make it very difficult to consistently attack. Also, the rubber doesn't have the grip to curve the ball to wide angles. Once you serve no-spin or light spin deep and fast, he will give you a high ball near the middle of the table. This is your chance; aggressively attack this ball! If he returns it, push the next ball. If you continue to loop consecutive balls, the backspin will accumulate and you will eventually miss. Remember, if you push, then the next ball will have slight topspin. If you loop, the next ball will have backspin.

Key Points
1. Kiss
2. Serve deep "no-spin"
3. Push deep
4. Loop one, push one—don't often attack two consecutive balls
5. Attack strong if the opportunity arises
6. Remember: Long pips and anti aren't confusing, your own spin is just coming back reversed

Day 34
Beat the One-Sided Player

Today, your opponent has one weak side and one strong side (forehand or backhand); of course, he wants to play his strength as much as possible regardless of how much he must move, lean, reach, and dive to use his strong side. There are several reasons that this player might not want to play the other side – it could be because of a physical limitation, an injury, or it might just be his preferred way to play and he hasn't developed both parts of his game equally. Also note that sometimes his weak side will have pips or anti as a crutch for that weakness.

In order to beat the one-sided player, you must first identify the weak side. A one-sided player is defined as someone who has a strong forehand and weak backhand or a strong backhand and a weak forehand. This style can first be most readily identified by looking at a player's stance. Generally if this one-sided player is standing square to the table (with both feet parallel to the table) he is a backhand player. If he is standing with the right foot back significantly (for a righty) then he is more forehand oriented. This can be a frustrating style to play against. For example, you are playing against a backhand blocker and no matter what you do, he just pushes and blocks on the entire table with his backhand. You must play long distances starting from the serve and first attack. For example, serve short angled wide to the forehand and then attack deep to the wide backhand; OR the opposite. Serve short angled wide to the backhand then attack deep to the wide forehand. In the longer rallies, it will be very difficult for this one-sided player to transition well from both forehand and backhand. He may also have unorthodox rubber; watch for racket flips throughout the point.

Key Points
1. Identify the weak side
2. Check the racket for an unorthodox rubber
3. Watch for racket flips
4. Play long distances—force him to use his weak side
5. Force him off the table
6. Play long rallies

Day 35
How to Beat a Wheelchair Player

Playing against a wheelchair player requires a specific strategy. (Much of what follows applies to a standing disabled player as well.) First, you must begin the match with a fighting spirit. If you start the match feeling sorry for your opponent, you probably won't give your best. Determine in your mind prior to the start of the match that you will give your very best and not worry about the sympathy factors. Some players go back and pick up every ball for the wheelchair player so that he doesn't need to wheel back for every ball. If you want to do it, that is very nice of you. However, for most players, it is a big distraction. If you are distracted by this, you can ask the tournament staff to provide you with an umpire or ball boy that can perform this task. I feel that you should be nice to the wheelchair player, but you should not be forced to retrieve every ball which takes you out of your normal rhythm.

Before the match begins, check the wheelchair player's racket to see what type of rubber he is using. Most wheelchair players use pips or anti.

When serving against a wheelchair player remember that the serve needs to go off the end of the table. If the wheelchair player feels that the serve is going at a wide angle off the side of the table, then he has the option to let the ball go. If he lets the ball go and does not play the rally and the ball goes off the side, then the point is a let. If he lets the ball go and does not play the rally and the ball goes off the end-line, then it is your point. So, don't feel unnecessary pressure that your serve needs to be in the exact center of the table. If your serve goes off the sideline, then the point is a let.

After the serve, you are allowed to play any ball anywhere on the table. Your serve return and your rally shots should normally go as wide as possible. Many players get stuck on the fact that they need to serve off the end; so they have the mindset for the rally and play all the balls down the middle. There is a huge advantage of using the angles during the rallies.

If you serve short and the wheelchair player cannot touch the ball, he is allowed to continue to let the ball bounce on his side of the table until the ball drops off the table. If the ball drops off the side of the table, then the point is a let. If the ball drops off the end of the table, then it is your point. Again, during a rally, you are allowed to hit the ball as short as you want or as wide as you want.

During the rally, try to vary the depth as much as possible. He probably plays very close to the table, so jamming him on the back line (near the body) should be your target. Also, very short topspin and no spin serves work well. If he pushes the serve, it should often give you an easy pop-up. If he leans clear over the table and flips the serve, then you can attack quickly and catch him leaning over the table. If you serve short backspin and he pushes back short, then try to use the angles on your push. If you serve long, try to serve deep to the elbow (the transition point between forehand and backhand). Many wheelchair players like to play about 70% backhand and only 30% forehand. So be prepared for their transition point to be slightly more to the forehand side of the table.

Remember that wheelchair players often play against standing opponents. However, standing opponents (like you) rarely play against wheelchair players. So be willing to take your time between points, look for weaknesses, and be willing to adjust your strategy based on what is working and what is not working.

Key Points
1. Play your best – don't easy off
2. Check his racket prior to the start of the match to see if he has unorthodox rubber
3. Get a ball boy
4. Use the angles during serve returns and rallies
5. Serve short no-spin or short topspin
6. Find his transition point
7. Jam him deep to the middle
8. Be prepared to adjust and re-adjust your strategy

Day 36
Beat the All-Around Player

This next opponent is difficult to put into a specific category, so we will call him the all-around player. He is usually quite consistent in pushing, blocking, and attacking. His goal is to keep long rallies in whatever manner it takes until you give him an easy ball. He often looks for your weaknesses and forms his strategies around attacking those areas.

So what do you need to do? First, decipher which style is working best for him and which style he is playing on this particular day. Although the all-around player can use any game style to win, he probably wins the majority of his points with one particular fashion. Second, be patient and wait for the right ball to attack. Third, aim to go for shots which will hit ninety percent of the time with good placement and variation. Your own consistency is a huge key. If the all-around player changes his strategy and begins winning, you may need to temporarily change your strategy accordingly.

Key Points
1. Decipher which style he is winning points with
2. Use good ball placement and variation
3. Be consistent and wait for the right ball to attack
4. Be prepared for him to change his strategy
5. Be flexible in your own strategy

Day 37
Beat the Short Pips Attacker

The short pips attacker wants to play quick attacks over the table. No matter if he attacks first or not, he wants to finish the point with quick, off-the-bounce attacks. He often serves long and fast, looking to smash your weak return.

So what do you need to do? You need to serve short and very low or possibly serve long if he doesn't attack the long serve. The KEY—don't open with an initial soft attack. If you attack soft, he will pips-out counterattack and put you running on your heels. Either attack strong and deep in the last nine to twelve inches of the table OR push deep. If you attack deep, the spin and depth will give the pips player a difficult time keeping the ball low. If you push heavy and deep with good placement, then he will likely roll the ball up, which is easy to counterattack. Also, when you loop wider angles, the pips player may have to move back from the table. The pips ball will have a very short trajectory; it is almost impossible for your opponent to attack consistently when away from the table.

Key Points
1. Attack strong and deep
2. Push deep
3. Counterattack his weak opening
4. Loop deep and spinny (last four inches of the table)
5. Play wide angles
6. Try to push him back from the table

Day 38
Beat the Seemiller-Grip Player

Here in the United States, the Seemiller grip aka "the American grip" is somewhat common among older players. There are three different versions of the grip, but we won't go into the details about the grip itself. We will look more closely at the strategy against this particular player. The main distinguishing factor is that this opponent only uses one side of the racket with both backhand and forehand. His racket is rotated slightly allowing him to play both forehand and backhand with the same side of the racket. For this reason, he might have an unorthodox rubber (like anti or long-pips) on the backside of the racket that he uses for blocking loops or returning serves. Make sure that you check his racket prior to the beginning of the match. Your opponent here probably wants to attack first from near the table. If he can't attack first, he will push to either deep corner then use his quick backhand block to move you. Instead of moving back and counterlooping, he will stay close and use an anti block as a slow variation.

    The Seemiller grip player is probably unable to consistently loop with his backhand. If you push deep to the backhand, you will probably get a deep push return. Because this opponent has a very limited range-of-motion with his wrist, he will have difficulty flipping your serve—even short topspin. Also, it is difficult for him to open his racket angle on the short backhand; so serve as short and wide with as much backspin as you can to his short backhand. Once the rally has begun, he likes to control the table with his backhand block, which has exceptionally good placement. Therefore, attacking the wide forehand will push him back and end his hopes of controlling with the backhand. As the match progresses, he might start looping with his forehand from the backhand side. For this reason, make sure that you surprise him with plenty of deep pushes to the forehand as well as long serves to the forehand. This will freeze him up from comfortably stepping around to use his forehand from the backhand side. As the match progresses, he also might start blocking more with his backhand from the middle or even the forehand side because he has more confidence with the backhand block. If this happens, try to also loop some balls to the wide backhand as a variation.

Key Points
1. Check his rubber before beginning the match
2. Attack to his wide forehand
3. Push to his deep backhand
4. Serve short topspin and be ready to loop his soft flip
5. Serve very heavy backspin short to the wide backhand
6. Play wide angles during the rallies to move him away from the table
7. Be ready for him to block many balls each rally
8. Watch for racket flips on serve return and when blocking

Day 39
Beat the Traditional Penholder

Your next opponent plays a traditional penhold style attacking strong with his forehand and blocking with his backhand. He tries to play most of the table with his forehand when attacking and has a particularly strong forehand when he uses it from the backhand side.

So what should you do against this difficult opponent? You need to attack very wide to his forehand so that you can force the penholder to hit the next ball with a weak backhand from off the table. After you serve, try to move the player to a long distance position from where the last ball was hit. For example, serve short angled wide to the forehand then attack deep to the wide backhand, or the opposite. Serve short angled wide to the backhand then attack deep to the wide forehand. If he won't turn and loop a deep push to the backhand, that's also a good option. If this particular penholder blocks a lot, you can also vary your loops by mixing high, spinny loops to the backhand. With this particular grip, it is somewhat difficult to block those high loops.

Key Points
1. Attack first
2. Loop powerfully to the forehand in order to move him back
3. If he moves back, attack backhand
4. Play long distances
5. Loop high and spinny to the backhand

Day 40
Beat the Girl

Competing in tournaments against girls is much different than competing in tournaments against guys. I have played against many top female players including Shen Yanfei, Wang Chen, Gao Jun, Chiharu Yamazaki, Mo Zhang, Watanabe Yuko, Jiaqi Zhang, and many other Olympic level female players. There are several tactics that I have learned from competing against them.

Most girls play quick-off-the-bounce counterdrives and smashes without much spin. They are used to hours and hours of counterdriving. If you stay close and play flat hitting against them, you have no chance to win. So, try your absolute best to play much differently than a girl would like to play. There are four main tactics that I would recommend that you use.

1. Use spin! Spinny serves work very well against girls because they aren't able to produce as much spin on their own. Previously, you learned about serve return – that by producing spin, the receiver can control the spinny serve much easier. Not only should you use spin on your serves, but you should use spin on your loops and pushes while keeping them low and deep. Your female opponent will easily smash your weak loop for a winner. So don't loop weak. If you can't give a good low, spinny loop, then don't loop – just push until the right moment.

2. Use Power! When you do decide to loop, the girl will probably try to smash your loop. If you are able to loop with good speed, it will be extremely risky for her to smash your loop. If she does consistently smash your loop, you should consider more variations in spin, speed, height, depth and placement.

3. Sometimes lob! Most girls don't train against lobbers. If you need to lob, you can probably win a decent percentage of the points just lobbing. Due to a lack of strength and technique, most girls do not have enough power to hit through a good lobber. As they fatigue, they will tend to use the drop-shot very often. If you see a drop shot, be ready to step forward for the attack. I would not recommend using lobbing as your Plan A. However, if your loop does get smashed, lobbing isn't a bad way to save the point.

4. Give extreme variations! Girls typically like to play patterns again and again and get into a smooth rhythm. Try to avoid a pattern like two balls to her backhand then one ball to the forehand. If she notices the pattern, she will be able to gear up her smashing game. By continually changing your shots from loops, to chops, to drop-shots, to lobs, you will be able to break her rhythm.

Day 41
Beat the Heavy-Weight Champ

When playing against an overweight opponent, there are a few things that you must remember.

1. Don't underestimate him based on his size.
2. Realize that he probably stays very close to the table.
3. Realize that he will likely have difficulty moving in-and-out.
4. Realize that he probably uses his wrist well and can be very deceptive with his shots.

With these four things in mind, start the match seriously and be respectful. If you mentally criticize your opponent because of his extra body weight, because of his strange clothes, or any other reason, you won't be able to fully concentrate on your strategy. Because he stays very close to the table, he will likely be able to cover the corners very well. Sometimes hitting the ball deep toward his belly is a great strategy. Surprisingly, he can probably reach and cover the angle balls fairly well, but he will likely have major problems when moving in-and-out. Most of the short game play involves not only stepping forward, but leaning forward. Without good core strength and posture, it will be very difficult for him to lean forward. Start with a very, very short no spin serve. After he flips, try to attack quick to the middle. Or, start with a very, very wide-angled backspin serve, and after he pushes, try to attack quick to the middle. Also realize that he likely has other strengths to compensate for his lack of mobility. Watch out for trick serves and deception in ball placement.

If you take this match seriously and apply these strategies, you will be well on your way to beating the heavy-weight champion!

Day 42
Beat the Lefty

Generalizing all lefties into one category is difficult, but I'll do my best to explain some general strategies that would apply to most lefties. I'm assuming that you (the reader) are right-handed.

Serve Return
When the lefty is serving a forehand serve from the backhand side, adjust your position slightly more to the right. The lefty will often use a sidespin serve to curve the ball away to your wide forehand. By standing more to the right, you will be able to better cover the wide forehand.

Down-the-Line Block
When looping to the lefty's backhand, be ready for him to block anywhere. If you have just played a ball from your wide forehand side of the table, he will probably try to block down-the-line quick to your backhand. Try to stay close to the table, hold your hand high, shorten your stroke, and backhand loop to a good location.

Expose the Forehand
By attacking to the wide forehand with your backhand, you will usually force the lefty to move slightly back from the table. This is exactly what you want! By moving him back, you will weaken his backhand and force him to play with a bigger court. Try to stay close and control the table after he backs up.

Higher Blocking
When playing a backhand loop against a righty's backhand block, the ball typically stays fairly low. When looping with your backhand against a lefty's forehand block, the ball often comes slightly higher because most players don't block as well or as low with the forehand. To adjust for his difference, start your backswing high and loop through the ball. If the block comes too high, you might consider stepping around to use a forehand on that ball.

Spin
When a lefty is serving sidespin, it is easiest to stop his forehand serve with your backhand and easiest to stop his backhand serve with your forehand. If you can't use the preferred side to receive, you might need to bend your wrist back slightly to deal with the heavy sidespin.

Soft and Hard
This lefty probably has a better backhand block and a better forehand counterloop. If you are stuck and forced to give a weak loop, then play to his middle or backhand. If you are in position and can play a powerful loop, I would recommend playing 60% of the time to his wide forehand, 20% of the time to his middle, and 20% of the time to his wide backhand.

Day 43
Beat Your Friends

Sometimes, beating your regular training partners, fellow club members, and best friends in table tennis can be very difficult because it seems that they know your every move. They can predict that your forehand flip will go crosscourt, they can predict that backhand serve will go long to the middle, and they can predict that you will block to the corners. They know your every move because they have played against you hundreds of times. There are two main solutions to overcome these problems:

#1: You must realize that you know your friend's game as well. Think about his common patters and develop strong strategies against these predictable patterns.

#2: You must be able to slightly adjust your shot selection and ball placement enough to mess him up. For example, if your backhand block usually goes first to the backhand, then to the wide forehand, then back to the backhand ... try to mix it up by blocking to the middle. If your forehand flip usually goes crosscourt to his forehand, try to slow the pace and play down-the-line instead. These subtle adjustments will really work. If your friend was playing against a total stranger, then he would be forced to really concentrate on where the next ball is going. However, he will assume that you will play as before and your changes will really throw him for a loop.

Day 44
How to Beat Yourself!

Players often strategize on how to beat their rivals. They spend endless hours studying video clips of the strategies that their opponents will be using against them. Instead of focusing merely on your opponent, try to get into your rival's head and think what he is thinking…
Write up a detailed game plan on how to beat yourself!
1. What are your main strengths and weaknesses?
2. What is your overall game style?
3. Where is your transition point when attacking?
4. Where is your transition point when defending?
5. What distance from the table do you prefer when attacking?
6. What distance from the table do you prefer when defending?
7. What are some common game patterns that you use?
8. What are some common game patterns that work against you?
9. What kinds of serves do you commonly use?
10. What kinds of serves give you trouble?
11. What is your preferred way to return serves?
12. What types of serve returns give you trouble?
13. What variations do you often use in the beginning of the match?
14. What tendencies do you have at the end of a close game?
15. What do you fall back on as Plan B when losing?
16. What do you fall back on as Plan C when losing?

Once you can think what your opponent is thinking … then you can have a clearer strategy on what you should be improving in your own game!

Chapter 6: Practice

Day 45
Effective Practice

A famous table tennis athlete once said, "If you practice as much as the world champion, you will be as good as the world champion!"

Is this a true or false statement?

I feel that it is false. Many players train for table tennis, but few train effectively. An effective training session consists of several elements: technique, duration, and intensity.

Technique
Hire a professional coach to analyze your game and help you make a list of improvements in order to reach the next level. These problem areas might be footwork, body balance, strokes, timing, etc. Have your list next to the table and review them before, during, and after each training session. I personally have twenty-three minor improvements and changes that I'm making in my game. Each day, I target a few of these areas. Improving my technique will be one of the key elements to boosting my game to the next level.

Duration
The length of your practice session will depend on your level and goals. I encourage each of my students to practice at least ten hours per week. Most of my top students take two hours of lessons per week as well as practice with the Newgy Robo-Pong 2050 four hours per week and play matches at the club four hours per week. Over a period of two years, many of my students have improved 500-1000 points. For elite players, it is necessary to practice about six hours per day to compete at the national level.

Intensity
If you are going to sink lots of time and money into your table tennis game, I hope that you would be focused for each session. Train hard! Train often! Results in tournament come from excellent practice sessions. Rank each session as good, better, and best. Keep track of your progress and give good focus on all aspects of the game for the best possible results.

Day 46
Plan A vs Plan B

If you are winning a match, then typically you will keep your tactics while making minor adjustments in your shot selection and giving some variations in your shots. If you are losing a match, then typically you will need to make more changes. If the match continues as it started, you will lose. So, you will need to decide to push yourself to make the necessary changes.

What kind of changes need to be made?

Plan A Changes
At the start of each match, you should have a game plan as to how you want to perform. Knowing yourself, you probably know which 5-6 serves best set up your game, which strengths that you want to use, and which patterns you commonly play. If you begin losing the match, then you need to tweak your first plan. Instead of merely serving the same serves, consider changing them slightly in spin, speed, depth, and placement. Instead of looping your normal way, consider adding more variations. Instead of blocking how you normally block, push yourself to do something different. Making those adjustments during the match

is necessary to change the momentum during a match.

Plan B Changes

As the same match progresses, you realize that making minor adjustments to Plan A really isn't working. So, you decide to go to Plan B. Plan B is a totally different game. Instead of playing your normal game, you completely adjust your style to go after your opponent's weaknesses. Let me illustrate: let's suppose that you are a looper who typically serves all short backspin serves and loops slow spinny consistent loops. You are playing against a blocker, who doesn't loop well, but can beat you with his quick blocks. Changing to Plan B might be to serve long, push long, and allow the blocker to loop first. Once he has looped first, you counterloop a winner. Although this isn't your main style, you give it a try because you are down 2-0 in games and losing 5-1 in the 3rd.

Generally, adjusting and re-adjusting your Plan A game is the safest tactic because it allows you to stay within your comfort zone while giving your opponent good variation. However, there are times when Plan A isn't working. Consider practicing your Plan B or even Plan C game at the club from time to time. You never know when it will be necessary.

Day 47
Disappointment

Sometimes players will work very hard over the summer training many hours each day. At the end of the summer, they play a tournament and are very disappointed with their results. They might have spent thousands of dollars traveling to China, hiring pro coaches, and giving great effort ... but still they didn't have the expected results.

Yet other times, players will take a break for a few weeks and practice very little. Without expecting much from their first tournament of the season, these players are sometimes surprised with amazing results!

So, why does this happen to so many players?

Actually, I think that there are several possible reasons...

1. Sometimes players who aren't expecting much are able to play worry-free, relaxed without effort. While others who have trained very hard put too many unnecessary expectations on themselves and the pressure hurts their performance.

2. Sometimes players who are training hard every day are making positive changes to their games – new strokes, new serves, and new strategies. Before these players can properly implement their new weapons, they first must play many practice matches and tournaments before perfecting these new elements. On the other hand, players who haven't been practicing much might not be so worried about the exact technique used.

3. Sometimes game styles have a huge impact into the performance of many players. If these players are matched up against ideal styles, they can play well. However, if they are matched up against difficult styles, these players may play poorly. For example, if a group of players practice speed work for six hours per day in China, they might have difficulty playing slow blockers or choppers.

Regardless of the outcome, these players must remember that practice is a necessary element to long-term major improvement. Just because they had one great performance after a four-week vacation, does NOT mean they will continue to have great tournaments without practice. Consistent practice while making positive changes with the help from a coach is the best way to improve long term.

Day 48
Practice Six Days

"So, Samson, how many days per week should I practice?" - That's a good question. If you don't practice enough, you won't be improving to your full potential. If you practice too much, you will likely get burned out or injured. At one point, China went to a longer workweek without giving days off ... and they weren't productive. In one particular country, at a national table tennis training center, the coach decided to do 28 days of practice, and then two days' rest. The players were getting injured and didn't have sufficient rest. I think that we see the best balance to this question in the Bible, Genesis 1:31-2:3

And God saw everything that he had made, and behold, it was very good. And there was evening and there was morning, the sixth day. Thus the heaven and the earth were finished, and all the host of them. And on the seventh day God finished his work that he had done, and he rested on the seventh day from all his work that he had done. So God blessed the seventh day and made it holy, because on it God rested from all his work that he had done in creation.

I think this is the perfect balance for table tennis and for life – six days of hard work and one day of rest. God made us. God designed us. God knows our bodies more than we could ever possibly know.

Day 49
What's Next?

I have been told that the Chinese players can think eight shots in advance. When they serve a particular serve, they can anticipate the next ball. They have an idea of what they will do next, then next, then next. I'm not going to suggest that you plan that much in advance; however, I would like for you to think at least one shot in advance. Today, I'm going to assume that you are an 1800-2200 level two-wing looper playing against your opponent who is another average 1800-2200 level two-wing looper. I'm going to outline your basic serves and give likely probabilities of the returns. (Please note: the probability will depend greatly on the quality of your serve, the confidence of your opponent, the type of rubber used, and other situations.)

You serve long backspin
- 80% of the time, your opponent will loop
- 15% of the time, your opponent will push long
- 5% of the time, your opponent will smash, lob, push short, or other returns

You serve long topspin
- 70% of the time, your opponent will loop or smash

- 20% of the time, your opponent will block
- 10% of the time, your opponent will lob, push short, push long, or other returns

You serve long no-spin or sidespin
- 60% of the time, your opponent will loop
- 20% of the time, your opponent will push long
- 20% of the time, your opponent will smash, lob, push short, or other returns

You serve short backspin
- 50% of the time, your opponent will push long
- 30% of the time, your opponent will push short
- 20% of the time, your opponent will flip, smash, lob, or other returns

You serve short topspin
- 80% of the time, your opponent will flip or smash
- 15% of the time, your opponent will push long
- 5% of the time, your opponent will push short, lob, or other returns

You serve short no-spin or sidespin
- 50% of the time, your opponent will flip
- 30% of the time, your opponent will push long
- 20% of the time, your opponent will push short, lob, or other returns

Once you can serve and have a general idea of the likely possible returns, it is then time to start thinking to yourself WHAT'S NEXT after that?
- After you push short to the middle, what might likely come next?
- After you loop to the wide forehand, what might likely come next?
- After you counterloop to the middle, what might likely come next?
- After you smash to the wide backhand, what might likely come next?

Day 50
The Attacking Mindset

If you are an offensive players, there are two aspects of the game that you need to master.

The first aspect is ... creating the opportunity to attack first. I hear many club players telling themselves throughout the night, "Just attack!" Well that sounds nice, but how are you going to create the opportunity. There are several ways.
1. Try to loop long serves
2. Try to loop half-long serves
3. Try to serve short and push short so that your opponent can't easily loop first
4. Try to loop most of the long pushes
5. Try to loop most of the flips

After you make the opening attack, try to continue attacking by following up with another ball and another ball. Against a good player, it will likely take 3-4 strong attacks to win the point.

The second aspect is ... being consistent in your attack. Even if you can create the opportunity to attack, that doesn't mean that you will win, that merely means that you have the ability to attack. You should target to make 80-90% of your attacks on with both your backhand and your forehand. If you are making 100% of your opening attacks on and still losing, then you possibly need to give more spin variation, speed variation, and placement variation. If you are inconsistent on your attacks, then consider adjusting your technique in the following ways.
1. Try to move into position better
2. Try to read the amount of spin that your opponent is giving you
3. Try to adjust the height of your backswing based on the spin and based on the height of the ball
4. Try to adjust the length of your swing based on the speed of the ball
5. Try to adjust your racket angle based on the spin on the ball
6. Try to focus on spin as your primary weapon and use speed as your secondary weapon

Day 51
Returning Nets and Edges

Many championship matches are won and lost on "lucky balls" – nets and edges. At the elite level, returning nets and edges is a skill that takes years to master. Today, I'm going to give several tips on how to safely land these balls.

Feet First
In table tennis, it is ideal to move into position and then swing. This seems very difficult to do. Sometimes you might be swinging as you move; however, the longer you keep your hand in front, the better balance you will have. Most club players have this reversed. Most club players try to reach the ball; then once they can't reach it, they lunge for it. If you are disciplined in moving and then swinging, you will have an easier time making the last minute adjustment with your hand.

Read the Spin
When the ball hits the net or edge, it maintains the same spin. For example, if your opponent loops at you, the ball has topspin. When it hits the net, it still has topspin; so make sure that you cover over the ball.

Over the Table
If you are returning a net ball, I would suggest contacting the ball over the table. Once the ball drops below the table, it is much more difficult to control.

Keep It Low
The most important part about returning nets and edges is keeping the ball low. If the ball is returned high, your opponent will probably smash. If you return low, your surprised opponent will be forced to make a difficult return.

Go For It
The best way to practice returning nets and edges is to ... Go For It! Every practice, every club night, every tournament gives you an opportunity to practice this skill. My mind is so engrained with reacting for the net ball that I even jump when watching a table tennis DVD. You too can train yourself if you put forth the effort. It's fun! Go for it!

Day 52
Slump Busting

At some point in your playing career, you have probably encountered a bad slump. How long will the slump last? Sometimes a day, a month, or a year. Today, I'm going to give you several tips on how to get out of a slump.

#1 Rest Your Mind
After a tough tournament or a sloppy practice session, sometimes it is good to rest your mind. Take off one or two days of training and do another activity, preferably an outdoor activity. Gazing at the stars, going to the mountains, and fishing by a waterfall are a few of the many things that help me relax the most.

#2 Re-evaluate Life
After a couple days rest, try to re-evaluate your life goals. I really like the Bible verse *Psalm 113:3 From the rising of the sun to its going down,*

the LORD's name is to be praised. Personally, my life goal is to praise God with everything – work, school, family, table tennis, and life. In the beginning of this book, I mentioned the expression, "If you don't know where you are going, any road will get you there." So, re-evaluate your life goals and know where you want to go.

#3 Re-evaluate Table Tennis
Next, re-evaluate your table tennis goals. Set a realistic long-term goal and then make small challenges to yourself of what you need to accomplish to reach the end goal. Continue to remind yourself that the road might be bumpy, but with the right coaching, training, and persistence, you can reach your goal.

#4 Timing is Everything
In about 90% of the cases, players go into slumps because of timing issues. In order to correct a timing problem, focus on keeping your racket in front longer. When a backspin ball approaches, move your feet quickly into position, but don't take your racket back until the ball has crossed the net by at least a few inches. Take your backswing just before the ball touches your side of the table. When a topspin ball approaches, move your feet quickly into position, but don't take your racket back until the ball has nearly reached the net. As the ball approaches, take your backswing back based on the incoming ball. For fast topspin, take a shorter swing. For slow topspin, take a longer swing while still contacting the ball in front of you. Most slump players try to take the same exact backswing for a topspin ball regardless of the speed, high, spin, trajectory, or contact point. Learning how to adjust your swing will greatly increase your timing!

#5 Consistency
Consistency is the main determining element to winning and losing matches. It doesn't matter if you are a marathon runner or a power lifter, if you cannot consistently return serves, loop the ball on the table, block loops, and other skills, then you will not win. Consistency is the key. If you are in a slump, consider how you can make your shots more consistent. Possibly you need to…
- Read the spin better when returning serves…
- Impart better spin on the ball when looping…
- Target placement on your push rather than power…

- Focus on relaxing your grip when blocking…
- Adjust with your feet better when smashing…
- And Take your time between points…
- If your consistency improves, winning will easily follow

#6 Advice
Be willing to admit to a table tennis friend that you are in a slump. Ask him to watch one of your club matches and give some advice based on what he sees. Sometimes it helps just having someone there to watch and encourage you.

#7 Coaching
Coaching is an absolute necessity. Before receiving professional advice, I was at the bottom of the barrel at the club, with nearly all losses, week after week after week after week. After two years of coaching, I improved 1000 points because the coach was able to take me where I couldn't take myself. I wasn't able to learn all the necessary elements to improving on my own; he taught them to me.

#8 Your Arsenal
While you are considering the suggestions above, you might want to also consider adding a new tool to your toolbox. The main part of winning is being consistent. The other part of winning is finding ways to make your opponent less consistent. By adding a new weapon to your arsenal, you could possibly make your opponent more uncomfortable and possibly win an extra 2-3 points each game. Consider learning a new serve, a blocking variation, a sidespin push, or a deceptive loop. If you are patient yet persistent, learning a new skill can be one of the best ways to start your new year and help you reach your end goal.

Day 53
Are You in a Jam?

After surveying dozens of club players across the country regarding game strategy, there is one common strategy used across the board. Most players work the point from corner to corner. Most players start off by playing against their opponents' backhands. If that doesn't work, then they play to the wide forehand then back to the backhand.

Only about 10% of the club players focus on playing the ball to their opponents' middle. When I use the term middle, I do not mean the white center line. The middle is the transition point between the forehand and backhand; this zone can really vary in location from player to player, but is usually roughly where the player's elbow is.

If you hit the ball to your opponent's backhand, he will usually react with a backhand, without thinking. If you hit the ball to your opponent's forehand, he will usually react with a forehand, without thinking. Both of those strokes flow naturally. However, when you hit the ball to your opponent's middle, he needs to make a quick decision, choose backhand or forehand, move into position, play the correct timing, then hit the ball. Once your opponent needs to make a "decision" his shot consistency and quality will be much worse. Even if he makes the shot on, it probably won't be quite as strong.

There are several drills that I do to help me play against my opponent's middle and help me when he plays against my middle. Let me give you an example of one of the drills.

In this drill, player A blocks with his backhand against player B's middle. The drill starts with player A serving to player B's middle and player B attacking with his forehand or backhand. If player B attacks with his backhand, then player A will block the next ball slightly more to the forehand side. If player B attacks with his forehand, then player A will block slightly more to the backhand side. Player A's goal is to force player B to feel uncomfortable by making him move and alternate between backhands and forehands. Player B's goal is to watch player A's racket, adjust with his feet, and maintain consistent attacks throughout the rally.

This same drill can be used by a blocker with the looper trying to pin the blocker at the transition point. After mastering the middle, the entire game will seem much easier and you will be able to flow from stroke to stroke with a smoother transition.

Day 54
Trajectories

In table tennis, you can contact the ball on the rise, on the top of the bounce, or on the fall. Sometimes beginners have difficulty controlling the spin, depth, and power because they don't know when to hit the ball.

If you are a beginner-intermediate player, I would recommend attacking from the top of the bounce, the highest point. This will allow you to have the most power hitting forward on the ball. If you attack on the rise or fall, then you need to lift somewhat. However, when defending (with push or block), I would recommend contacting the ball on the rise. By contacting the ball on the rise, it is easy to keep the ball low and control the ball. This is especially important when pushing short serves. When pushing, contact the ball early to keep it short or push quick as a surprise. When flipping, allow the ball to reach its peak in order to get maximum speed on your flip.

If you are an advanced player, you should be able to hit nearly every shot from every height. It is vitally important to practice at multiple distances to add more variation. However, you should have one main distance that you prefer and feel comfortable playing for each shot.

Day 55
Video Analysis

What are you looking at?

When watching a professional player, what you are looking at? Are you looking at the bright color of his shoes, the weird design on his shirt, his massive leg muscles, or the funny expression that he makes when serving? If so, you aren't studying the right things.

When watching a professional player, there are several things that you should be looking at…

1. **Preparation**
   Watch how he goes through his pre-point routine before stepping up to the table.

2. **Serve and Receive**
   Watch how he stands to receive serve – his distance from the table, his racket position, his racket height, his foot positioning, and his balance. Watch when he serves – his positioning, his backswing, his contact point, his follow through, and his return to the ready position.

3. **Footwork**
   Watch how he moves for each ball, watch how he anticipates for the next ball, watch how he continues to adjust and re-adjust for each ball with large leaps as well as micro steps.

4. **Shot Selection**
   Watch how he chooses when to loop, when to block, when to counter-loop, when to stay close, when to back up – watch his shot selection.

5. **Time Between Points**
   Watch how he takes his time between points. Watch as he walks back to pick up the ball how his body language is showing his thoughtfulness as he mentally gears up for the next point.

Instead of trying to watch all of these elements at once, I would recommend watching a short Youtube video five times. Each time, watch a different aspect of the game as outlined above. By training yourself to watch each aspect separately, you will better be able to learn the details of the sport.

Day 56
Five Ways to Dominate

In table tennis, there are five different ways that world class players win points. As you read these five points, ask yourself how well you are doing in each point.
1. Speed
2. Spin
3. Placement
4. Variation
5. Consistency

Ma Long wins most of his points with speed and consistency. Ma Lin wins many points with speed and spin. Waldner wins many points with variation and placement. Rye Seung Min wins many points with speed. Wang Zhen wins many points with consistency and variation. Professional players each have their own unique style. However, if they begin losing, they adjust their game strategy and use another elements to win points. For example, if Timo Boll starts the match winning many points with the spin on his serve and spin on his loop, then he continues to use the same strategy. If he starts losing, he must re-evaluate his game and choose another aspect to focus on.

- Maybe he could continue to use the same strategy but improve his placement...
- Maybe he could push himself to attack earlier and play more power...
- Maybe he could vary his spin more and vary his shot selection more...
- Maybe he could continue the same strategy and focus on being more consistent...

Before you begin a match, you should consider the five elements listed above. Think about what will be your main way to win points against this particular opponent. Throughout the match, be willing to adjust and readjust your strategy. If you can learn to win points with a good blend of all five elements, you will be a complete player and be able to adjust to any opponent.

Chapter 7: Tournaments

Day 57
Tournament Tough

As we begin this intense chapter, I would like to share with you twenty general tips on how to be tournament tough. During the course of the next few days, you will be learning additional details that will boost your tournament play.

1. **Prep work: Set goals**
   Setting a goal is the first step in becoming tournament tough. Goal setting should happen a few months prior to the tournament. Write out your goal and post it in your training room. With this goal in mind, next determine how to properly prepare to meet that goal – what you should be practicing, what changes you should be making, who you should be practicing with, how often you should be playing matches, what you need to do nutritionally, and what you need to do in physical preparation. Be specific in regards to your target goal and be specific in regards to your preparation to meet that goal.

2. **Prep work: Know yourself**
   Reflect back to prior performances and ask yourself about what you did right and what you did wrong. Make a plan and train for a couple months to fix your problems and strengthen your strengths. If you can't clearly remember, then watch video clips and analyze the video.

3. **Prep work: Prepare yourself**
   Now that you know what you need to do, spend the time before

the event preparing. Months before the event, you will be making changes in your game as well as building up your physical strength and speed. In the final week of the tournament, don't make major changes but instead ... continue to give yourself gentle reminders on the right things to do. Think back to previous successful tournaments, and rest and train appropriately to what works best for you. Some players need more practice (like myself) while other prefer more rest. Some players need more sleep (I prefer 8-9 hours) while others prefer normal sleep. Some players prefer more or less physical training. Some players prefer newer rubber (2-3 days old) while others prefer older rubber (1-2 months old). By properly knowing yourself and preparing yourself, you will have the best chance for success.

4. **Prep work: Know the tournament**
   Picture yourself walking in to the tournament. Picture the tables, floor, walls, lighting, and all the other conditions. Mentally put yourself in that moment. If you have never been to that facility before, then ask around about the conditions and playing format.

5. **Prep work: Prepare for the tournament**
   Preparing for the tournament also involves playing in similar conditions. If the lighting is dark, then consider turning off half the lights in your training room. If the walls are white and the balls are white, then consider putting a white tarp or drop sheet behind your training partner while using white balls. If you know that the tables are faster than normal, then train your short serves to be three bounces instead of two bounces. Do as much as you can to train in the same conditions as you will be competing in during the tournament.

6. **Prep work: Know the opponent**
   About 1-2 weeks before the tournament, try to find out who you might possibly be playing against. Many tournaments now have the player listing on Omnipong.com. As you are driving to the table tennis club to practice each night, spend a few minutes reflecting on what those opponents did last time they played against you – how they served, how they received, strengths, weaknesses, tendencies. If you don't know your opponent, then try to watch

Youtube videos or ask a friend at the club who might know him.

7. **Prep work: Strategize for the opponent**
Take out a pen and paper and write ten points on how your opponent wants to win points. Then write down ten points on what you should do against him.

8. **Prep work: Watch the opponent**
At the tournament, spend time watching your opponent. Even though you have a general strategy, this strategy might be drastically different if he has changed his playing style. See if he plays differently than before, see if he has any new serves, see if you can notice any additional strengths and weaknesses than you previously noticed.

9. **Prep work: Know who to talk with**
At tournaments, there are some players who are very negative – always complaining about something. There are other players who are very encouraging. These players want to help you prepare for a match, they also might coach you during the match, and they also might be able to give you comforting words after a match. These are the types of players to hang around with at tournaments. Attitudes are contagious.

10. **Game: Returning short serves with variation**
The most important thing in serve return is to return the ball onto the table. Generally, the safest way to return short serves is with a controlled push. Once you are able to properly read the spin and return those serves, it is now time to return short serves with some variation. There are three main ways to return short serves – with a flip, with a fast long push, and with a short push. When flipping short serves, placement is the key. With only about 5-6 feet to react to your flip, it will be very difficult for your opponent to properly react and stroke the ball if your placement is deceptive. To flip, step forward quickly, let the ball rise to the peak or even drop very slightly, brush the ball up and forward like a mini-loop over the table, then prepare by moving back quickly into position. To push long, step forward and push the ball quick off the bounce while following through the ball at least 8". When pushing long,

quickness is the key – not ball speed. By contacting the ball on the rise, you can take away the reaction time from your opponent while keeping it low and spinny. To push short, still you will step forward, stop your body movement, and take the ball on the rise. Instead of pushing deep though the ball, you will almost completely stop your swing and follow through about 2". After pushing short, then return back quickly to loop. If your opponent receives short back, then be ready to move forward again in order to push or flip.

11. **Game: Returning medium serves with variation**
Many players try to serve short, but many of their serves are actually medium-long. There are two options to returning a medium long serve – push or loop. If you choose to push, realize that it is very difficult to push short from a medium-long serve; so you will likely be forced to push long. With this long push, focus on placement. A better option would be to loop this serve. Your opponent probably thought that his serve was short. If you are able to loop the serve, then he will likely be very surprised and very disgusted by his poor serve. If his serve is backspin, then let the ball drop slightly off the end of the table, while spinning up and slightly forward with an open angle. If his serve is no-spin, sidespin, or topspin, then loop over the table with a slightly more closed racket. When looping the medium-long serve, you should be focusing on spin while keeping the ball low and deep with good placement.

12. **Game: Returning long serves with variation**
No matter how deceptive or fast your hit is, it must return on the table. In order to win a match, it is essential that you return their serves with at least 80-95% accuracy. If you are more accurate than 95%, then you can feel comfortable going for more risk with spin variation, speed variation, placement, and deception. When returning long serves, your most important duty is to apply spin. Spin allows you to control the ball. All world-class players loop or chop all long serves. You will never see a top player blocking a long serve. In order to chop or loop a long serve, give yourself plenty of distance from the table (about a full arm-length). When you are surprised by the long serve, quickly move into position, allow the ball to come fairly deep, and spin the ball with a loop or

chop. Unless you have very good spin on your loops, it is very difficult to loop a spinny serve off the bounce.

13. **Game: Relying on your strengths**
   Each player must have a couple very strong strengths that he can count on to win points ... possibly a good serve, a powerful smash, or a spinny loop. Try to develop some good serves and returns that best set up your strengths.

14. **Game: Dealing with your weaknesses**
   You must first understand your weak points. Once you understand your weak points, you need to improve them and be willing to sometimes cover them up. For example, if your backhand loop against push is a weak point, what can you do? Well, you can develop a good push with your backhand to keep you in the point. Or, you could develop strong footwork so that you can pivot and play a forehand from the backhand side. Or, you could develop a backhand loop. Think about all of your weak points and assume that your opponents will know your weak points. Plan on your opponents playing to your weak points and have a plan on what to do.

15. **Game: Have multiple serve weapons**
   With a very similar motion, it is important that you be able to produce various spins and serve to various locations. Try to have only 1-2 main serves that you use with 10-15 possible variations. You should also spend time practicing your attack after your serve. You should understand the ins and outs of what your opponent can possibly do with each of your serves.

16. **Game: Have multiple attack weapons**
   When looping, flipping, or smashing, it is essential that you be able to impart various spins on the ball, hit with various speeds, and target various locations. With a good change of pace, you can keep the winning momentum. It is also important to be able to adjust your loop to various spins. You must be able to loop against a light push, heavy push, flip, block, and many other types of balls. In order to properly do this, your loop must be adjustable and flexible.

17. **Game: Have a solid, consistent defense**
    When you are in a defensive position like pushing, blocking, or chopping, you must remain consistent and be able to lengthen the rally. If you are able to block back 4-5 of your opponent's loops, then you have a very good chance to win the point. With defense ... consistency and placement are the two keys.

18. **Mental: Enjoy the competition**
    In the fifth game, you developed a 9-3 lead. With some momentum, your opponent was able to come back and the score is now 9-9. How do you feel? Are you afraid? Afraid of what others might think? Afraid of losing rating points? Afraid of being eliminated from the tournament? Champions love the competition and love the feeling of a good exciting game. You will learn to play without fear when you learn to enjoy the competition instead of fearing the competition.

19. **Mental: Overcome Obstacles**
    Obstacles are a major part of every tournament. You forgot to bring your tt shoes! Ouch! You are getting called as having an illegal serve! Ouch! You haven't eaten lunch and your stomach is growling! Ouch! There are problems that all players must face. Before going to the tournament, try to deal with these anticipated problems. Realize that at the tournament there will be some surprises. At that point, it isn't a matter of what happened, it's a matter of how you deal with what happened.

20. **Post-Game: Reflection Time**
    After the tournament has concluded, you need to spend a couple hours thinking back to each match. Think deeply about what you did right and what you did wrong. Think back to one month prior to the tournament. If you could prepare for that tournament again, what would you do differently? Your answer should determine how you train this month in preparation for the next tournament.

Day 58
Coaching at Tournaments

Part I: You as the Coach

When coaching a friend, club member, or teammate in tournaments there are a few things to remember. First, try to be positive and encouraging to him. Even if your player has played poorly, try to find something encouraging to say while still giving solid advice. Next, try to keep your advice to 0-2 things. If he wins easily, you probably shouldn't say much of anything. If he plays poorly, then you can give 1-2 short pieces of advice. The advice should be in relation to the opponent. Most players understand that they are missing backhands or can't serve short. But the best advice should be as it relates to the other player – his strengths, his weaknesses, his serves, his tendencies, his patterns, etc. Also, be willing to listen. Sometimes students have questions or problems that need solved – so be a listening ear.

Part II: You as the Student

I recommend only receiving advice from players who know your game and have coached you in the past. If the player doesn't know the details of your game, then you are probably in for an arguing match, which doesn't put you in a winning frame of mind. If you have a coach who has helped you in the past and is knowledgeable about your strategy, it can be a wonderful winning combination. Before the match, you should briefly talk with your coach about the strategies related to that opponent. You should give your coach a note card with several key points that you want to remember and ask your coach to give his own advice as well as remind you about some of the points on your card. Between games, there should be a short 5-10 seconds of reflection from you. Next, the coach should talk for 15-30 seconds. Then there should be about 15-20 seconds of quiet and rest. After the match, you should have a few minutes to recover, a brief time of discussion about the match, then a brief time of focus for the next match.

Part III: You as the Forced Student

Unfortunately, there are times when you are forced to receive coaching from someone who doesn't know your game. If you are on the Olympic team, then you will obviously receive coaching from the Olympic coach, even if he isn't your primary coach. If you are playing at the NA Teams, then you will probably receiving coaching from your teammates, even if they aren't the ideal coaches. There will be times in your playing career that you will be coached by someone who you don't agree with or someone who doesn't know your game. What should you do?

1. Prior to the tournament, do everything possible to change coaches. If that isn't possible, then follow the rest of the steps.
2. A few days before the tournament, e-mail your soon-to-be-coach some videos of yourself playing. Explain your strengths, weaknesses, patterns, tendencies, and how your game has been progressing. Let the coach know your goals as well as your training routines and warm-up routines.
3. On the tournament day, have a brief moment with the coach explaining how you are feeling and discussing some strategies for known opponents.
4. As you begin your first match, give your coach a note card with some self-reminders about your specific strategies for that opponent.
5. Between games, don't argue with your coach. Listen patiently and don't force your opinion on your coach. You can try to clarify his advice, but don't argue with him. If he gives you very, very, very bad advice, I would recommend not obeying. Ultimately it is your responsibility to win the match, not your coach's responsibility.
6. After the match, thank the coach for his effort and communicate with him some of the positives and negatives about the match.

Day 59
Learn What???

    In order to maximize your performance, it is important that you learn <u>how to win</u> and that you learn <u>how to lose</u>. You might be thinking to yourself, "Samson, if you saw me at the last tournament, then you would say that I already have enough experience losing!!!" Actually, that's not what you will be learning today…

What you will be learning about today is the post analysis of a match. Sitting down in the bleachers after an awesome win and knowing what to do next. OR … Sitting down in the bleachers after a terrible loss and knowing what to do next.

How to Win

1. Keep in mind that just because you won the match, it doesn't make you a better person. Many times, high-rated players look down on recreational players as if they are the scum of the earth. You must first remember to treat your opponent with respect.
2. If you played an awesome match, remember what you did differently in this match than previously in other matches. Remember what you did RIGHT! Many of the days in your table tennis journey thus far have been geared around what you did wrong to correct it. Now, I want you to focus your attention on what you did RIGHT. Were you moving better? Were you spinning more? Were you placing the ball well? Were you looking for the first attack? Were you giving good speed and spin variations?
3. Finally, regain your focus for the next match. Often after a great win, you might not go into the next match with the best focus.

Remember, each opponent is different. You might need to have a slightly different strategy against the next player.

How to Lose

1. Keep table tennis in perspective. Character should come first. Winning or losing is not a life and death issue. After a hard loss, try to briefly leave the gym and clear your mind and think about something else for a few minutes – listen to relaxing music, go for a light jog, or play a video game – do something to distract you.
2. Understand that losing will help you more than winning. When you win, you probably don't learn much about your game – besides the fact that you are absolutely awesome! ☺ When you lose, it clearly shows you your flaws and you have more knowledge about what you should change in your training routine.
3. Come back with more determination on your next match. Come back for your next match with a renewed focus – be ready to make quick adjustments and do your best to apply your strategy. One loss in a tournament probably won't ruin you. However, if you lose your focus and your desire to fight … then you will continue to play poorly and continue to lose.

Day 60
Jet Lag

If you are a tournament player, jet lag can be one of your biggest enemies. I have a few recommendations on how to overcome this opponent...

1. Get plenty of rest before your trip. If you are rested ahead of time, losing 1-2 nights of sleep won't be as traumatizing.
2. Arrive early. If you arrive 2-3 days before the competition, then you will have time to recover and perform well.
3. Don't take naps. Once you have arrived at your destination, don't take naps during the day. A nap in the afternoon will be sure to mess up your sleep schedule. Instead of napping, try to go to bed around 9pm and sleep until 7am.
4. Don't think about it. If you didn't get much sleep the night before, don't dwell on it too much during the tournament – it will lead to negative thinking. If you didn't sleep much, you still must perform and still must give your best. Personally, I have played some of my best matches after only getting 2-3 hours of sleep the night before. Rest is important, but even without it, you can still perform! Just stay positive!

Day 61
Lucky Loser

If you have ever played a world pro tour event, you are probably familiar with the term "lucky loser." So what does it mean?

A lucky loser is a player who loses in an event but still advances due to an opening in the draw. For example, if there are 152 players entered in one pro tour event, there might be 32 players seeded into the single elimination and 120 players competing in round robin groups. There would be 30 groups of 4 players per group with the winners advancing to meet the 32 seeded players.

To form a perfect single elimination draw, there should be 64 players. After the groups finished, there would be 62 players remaining in the tournament – 32 seeded players and 30 qualifiers. To meet the perfect 64 number, the tournament referee would put the names of the 30 second-place finishers in a hat and draw 2 names. They call these players ... "lucky losers." They lost in the groups but were still able to advance and keep playing.

So, the next time that you are playing in a world pro tour and hear the phrase "lucky loser" you will perfectly understand what it means.

Day 62
Get Serious in the Morning

You were the top seed in the under 2300 event. Based on the draw, you knew that you didn't have a strong opponent on your opening 9am match; in fact, he was only rated 1600. You woke up at 8:25am and drove to the venue at 8:55am. You figured that after your opening match, that you would grab some breakfast and then begin your full warm-up for your 11am match. After dropping the first game, you decided that it was just your opening match and you would snap out of it. You thought that it would still be an easy 3-1 win. At the close of the second game, your opponent did the unthinkable. He scored 4 consecutive points with 3 net balls and an edge ball. Now, you were down 2-0 in games and your nerves got the best of you. Your morning wake-up call? Well, it was more than a wakeup call, it was the worst loss of your life! So how could you have prevented it?

#1 Serious
You needed to take that match serious, even when your opponent was rated much below you. By waking up early enough to eat a good breakfast, by jogging and stretching, by playing a few practice matches,

by doing a bit of research on your opponent, and by mentally gearing up prior to the match, you should have given your best from the very first hit! For future tournaments, you need to learn to be serious and give your opponent the needed respect.

#2 Fear
After losing the first game, you should have had some fear. Instead of taking the match seriously, you just dismissed it as an early morning match that would turn out fine in the end. Instead, you should fear losing. This fear of losing would have driven you to give 100% focus and to evaluate your opponent and possibly change your tactics. Some types of fear are good.

#3 Learn
Walking off the court after losing the match 3-0, you should have learned on how to deal with your loss. So what did you do next???... Quit? Mope around the tournament complaining? Follow your opponent around hoping that his rating gets adjusted? What did you do? I suggest that you should learn from that match and move forward. Think back to the match in regards to a strategy change for the next match but DON'T think back to the match in a depressing way. Use that match as fuel to energize your performance in future matches!

Day 63
Playing Higher Events

In tournaments, many players want to play in higher-rated events. Many 1200 players like to play in the u1800 and u2000 events. Many 1800 players like to play in the u2300 and u2500 events. Playing in these high-rated events can be beneficial or it can be harmful. Here are some benefits and risks…

Benefits: If you are training hard on a daily basis and making great progress, it is sometimes very good to play high-rated events. It will give you a clear picture on how the higher players perform and it will give you a test to see if you have been practicing effectively. Take time between each game to write statistics on your opponents and write his strengths and weaknesses. After losing a match to a very high-rated opponent, write down 5-10 ways that you need to improve if you want to someday reach that level. Again, if you are training hard and making great progress, then playing high players will give you a good goal of what you need to do.

Risks: If you are merely trying to improve your rating, then playing high-events is sometimes detrimental. Instead of trying to strategize on how to reach that level and how to improve to get to that level, you might be merely hoping to have one great win that will boost your level. Hoping for a win is not a way to major improvement. Hoping that your opponent will play poorly is also not a way to major improvement. Hoping to merely boost your rating without boosting your level is also not a way to major improvement.

For my personal students, I recommend that they try to play 10-15 matches on a tournament day. I suggest that they enter both lower and higher events. The lower events will push them to win matches at their level. The higher events will give them a goal to work toward.

Day 64
Scouting

Whether you want to make the US Olympic Team, win the senior games, or beat your Uncle Bob, it is always a great idea to scout out your competition. I'm going to describe two separate methods of scouting your opponent. The first is the long-term method. This is best accomplished by video analysis. The second is short term; this is a more common situation. You enter a tournament and are watching your opponent play the round robin group ten minutes before your match against him. You have never seen him before, and you need to quickly make a game-plan.

How to Scout an Opponent, Long-Term
Serve
When studying an opponent, the first thing to watch is his serve. Watch the motion, the bounce, how the ball reacts off the table, and how the ball reacts off the opponent's racket. Obviously, when watching, you can't "feel" the spin, but you can get "a feel" for the types of serves that he will probably serve against you. If possible,

watch a video of him playing against you or against someone who has a similar style and level to yours.

Serve Return
Next, study how this opponent returns serve by asking yourself the following questions.
1. Does he attack long serves with both forehand and backhand?
    If so, with what stroke? If not, how does he return them?
2. Does he attack short serves with both forehand and backhand?
    If so, what location does he usually attack to? If not, does he return long or short?
3. Are there any particular serves that he misses repetitively?

How He Wins Points
This point is slightly more general. Does he win most of his points by attacking or by allowing his opponent to attack first? If he wins most of his points by attacking, find out his biggest weapons and try to stop them. If he wins most of his points from his opponent missing, then try to be very consistent, eliminate your own errors, and choose the right ball to hit strong.

Specific Strengths
Now let's discuss in more detail about his strengths. First, check his stance. Is he in a forehand stance or backhand stance? Second, check his grip. Does he have a forehand grip (top of racket rotated to the thumb side of the palm) or a backhand grip (top of racket rotated to the index finger side of the palm)? Third, check his footwork. Does he move better to the forehand side or to the backhand side? When moving wide, does he move back or stay close to the table?

Specific Weaknesses
His weaknesses might be very evident. However, it is a good idea to analyze one or two full games and mark each time he misses with a particular stroke. For example:
- Forehand loop against underspin I
- Backhand loop against underspin IIIIII
- Forehand loop against topspin

- Backhand loop against topspin I
- Backhand push III
- Forehand push IIIIII
- Forehand block II
- Backhand block I
- Smash I

By looking at the statistics, you can clearly see that he missed many forehand pushes and many backhand loops against underspin. This will give you an indication that those might be two of his biggest weaknesses.

Game Patterns
Most game patterns happen in the first three shots. Watch how your opponent uses his serve to set up a great loop, an easy smash, or a well-placed block. If he does have patterns that he wants to play, you need to be aware of them and have game-plans on how to stop his winning routine.

End Game
At the end of a tight match, your opponent might change his game slightly –
- He might play more risky by playing extra power.
- He might play less risky by reverting to a push/block game.
- He might pull out a secret serve that he was saving the entire match.
- He might tighten up and feel nervous to use their backhand or forehand.
- He might call an umpire or try to cause controversy.

Regardless of what happens, you need to be aware of their tendencies. Be ready to keep your opponent off-guard and be ready to adjust to his changes.

How to Scout an Opponent, Short-Term

When playing in a tournament, you sometimes will have a very short notice on who your next opponent will be. In this case, try to watch him play a match in the previous round or in the round robin group. With only a few minutes to watch, I suggest that you focus your attention on two things:
1. His serve
2. How he wins points

Envision yourself playing him. Watch the serve, then immediately question yourself as to what the best return would be. See how his opponent returned the serve and confirm your answer by watching how the ball reacts off his racket. It is very important to watch the subtle differences that he makes in varying the spin with the same motion.

See how he wins points. Does he win most of his points by forceful attacking? Or does he win most of his points by allowing his opponent to miss? Once you have these two things solved, you will be thinking clearly when you formulate a pre-game strategy against this opponent.

Also, be willing to ask a friend or other players in the round robin group. His last opponent might be able to give you insight that you hadn't foreseen.

Day 65
The Statistics

At a professional tournament, statistics were taken for the length of the rallies. These statistics are fairly common across the board for all levels but differ based on game-style.

On average...
- 12% of serves are not returned
- 18% of points are won on the 2nd ball
- 26% of points are won on the 3rd ball
- 13% of points are won on the 4th ball
- 11% of points are won on the 5th ball
- 6% of points are won on the 6th ball
- 4% of points are won on the 7th ball
- 10% of points are won after the 7th ball

So as you can see, the serve, serve return, and 3rd ball attack are critically important ... 56% of the points do not last more than the 3rd hit. For this reason, I would recommend practicing at least 56% of the time on the serve, serve return, and 3rd hit.

Serve

One of the best ways to improve your serve is to do it during a drill. Instead of starting the drill with a warmup serve, start each drill with a tournament serve such as short backspin. Ask your training partner to push long, next you loop the push, then you begin the footwork drill.

Serve Return

You probably have some serves that give you problems. Ask your training partner to serve those problem serves again and again while thinking of new ways to return them. Experiment by attacking slightly stronger or slightly slower, by pushing instead of looping, by adding to or stopping the sidespin, or countless of types of returns. In order to properly read the spin on a serve, you should watch the racket motion, listen to the contact, watch the bounce, and look for the logo on the ball.

The Third Ball

Even if your opponent doesn't miss your serve, he might give you an easy return in which you can attack. If your 3rd ball attack is strong, it will put more pressure on your opponent to return more precisely. When he tries to return shorter or lower or faster, he will begin making more mistakes. Remember, it isn't just about your serve ... It's also about what comes after your serve.

Day 66
The Two Minute Warm-Up

   During a two-minute warm-up there are a few important things that you should be doing...

1. You should remove any distractions. If there is a barrier too close to the table and needs to be moved, adjust the barriers prior to the first point. If there are broken balls on the floor or dirt on the table, make sure that you clean the area.

2. You should get a good feel for the ball, table, floor, and lighting. By controlling the ball and looping with spin, not speed, you should develop a consistent, confident feel for the ball.

3. You should practice watching the ball as it approaches your racket, and then watch your opponent's racket as the ball is traveling toward your opponent. Most players merely watch the ball. Being able to watch your opponent's racket is also important because it give you a huge clue as to where he is planning to hit the next ball.

4. You should warm-up your footwork by making mini-steps during practice. Most players cannot hit the exact same spot on the table during practice. Instead of mentally complaining about the terrible warm-up, use it as a time to practice your short footwork. Be ready to adjust slightly in-and-out and side-to-side throughout the two-minute warm-up.

5. You should be studying your opponent's game style – his spin (or lack of spin), his grip, his stance, his strokes, and his overall game style. Especially if you have not seen him play previously, it is vitally important that you form a general picture of your opponent. As the match progresses, be willing to drastically change your strategy, if need be.

You should be reminding yourself of your tactics and encouraging yourself to do the right things. Regardless of who you are playing against, you probably have a couple of short sentences that you remind yourself of before every point. Even in practice, get in the habit of reminding yourself of the same things to get your mind in the game from the very first point.

Day 67
Checklist

When playing at a local table tennis club, you probably need your racket and shoes. However, there are some other items that you might want to include when traveling to a tournament. Below is a list of items that I generally bring:

- Racket
- Shoes
- Spare racket – identical and assembled
- Extra rubber
- Balls
- Video camera
- Extra batteries
- Tripod
- Hand towel
- Floor towel
- Glue
- Glue sponge applicator
- Scissors
- Net checker
- Snacks
- Drinks
- Money
- USATT membership card
- USATT rule book
- Tournament director contact info
- Directions to the venue
- Map
- Entry form, including event format and start times
- Notebook and pen
- Clothes

Tournaments add plenty of stress to the competitors. Having all the necessary items will just make it more enjoyable and less stressful. Remember while flying to keep your racket and shoes with you in your carry-on bag. Store other items (glue, scissors, etc.) in your checked luggage. Compete, enjoy, and don't forget the necessities!

Day 68
Kids

Kids love table tennis. Even starting as young as five years old, kids love the excitement. Many parents don't see the benefit. They must realize that table tennis training develops character.

I hear many coaches trying to convince the parents to have their kids take lessons because the kids can travel the world or get a nice college scholarship, or become a pro player in Europe. These things sound good on the surface, but many parents would still rather put their children into baseball or basketball.

Training and competing in table tennis actually develops character as I will describe in the following paragraphs.

Table tennis teaches kids how to work hard.
Table tennis takes hard work physically and mentally. No one reaches an elite level in a week or a month. It takes consistent hard work over ten years to develop to the top-level game. This hard work will carry over to other areas of life, even college or career.

Table tennis teaches kids about physical fitness and diet.
Fitness on and off the court is a daily routine for the top player. Developing good fitness and diet habits will last a lifetime and change a player for the rest of his life.

Table tennis teaches kids about success and failure.
Unfortunately, life is full of both success and failure. How should a player react when losing? How should he react when things aren't going his way? These same lessons will help him mature throughout his teen years.

Table tennis teaches kids about marketing.
In order to fund travel and training, many students need to learn to market themselves. Kids will learn how to talk to sponsors and how to best promote table tennis products.

Table tennis teaches kids how to handle pressure.
Many players can practice well but can't convert it to matches. The coach will teach the students what to think between points, how to react to good and bad points, how to handle conflict, and how to think clearly even in a pressure situation. This is vitally important for any career whether it be a job interview, a speech, or any other public job.

    Table tennis really does benefit other areas of life. The habits developed early will influence a child for the rest of his life.

Day 69
When to Complain

In the US, most tournament matches are not umpired. However, you can request an umpire if there is a problem. So when should you seek help from a tournament official? You should get help when your opponent is getting an unfair advantage from something like his serve.

Get an umpire if...
1. Your opponent is throwing the ball into the racket and getting an unfair advantage
2. Your opponent is hiding the ball and getting an unfair advantage
3. Your opponent is spinning the ball with his fingers and getting an unfair advantage
4. Your opponent is throwing the ball back excessively and getting an unfair advantage

Don't get an umpire if...
1. Your opponent is tossing the ball 4" instead of 6" (there is no advantage for him)
2. Your opponent is cupping the ball (there is no advantage for him)
3. Your opponent is putting the ball in his fingers instead of his palm (there is no advantage for him)
4. Your opponent is tossing the ball over the table by 1" (there is no advantage for him)
5. Your opponent is dropping the ball under the table by 1" (there is no advantage for him)

You should not complain just to complain ... and you should not complain just to break an opponent's momentum. However, if he is truly winning points from his illegal whatever, then you have the right to get help from an official. Also, it is important that you mention something in a gentle tone. Instead of calling your opponent a cheater, you might just mention to him that there is a problem (specify) that he might not be aware of and you feel the need to get an official.

In Proverbs 15:1 it says, "A soft answer turns away wrath, but grievous words stir up anger."

Day 70
You Can't Stop Him

Your opponent is attacking your short serve and you are frustrated that you can't stop him from attacking your serve. What should you do? Well, you must realize that with modern equipment and modern strokes, he will likely be able to attack all of your serves, regardless of how spinny, how low, and how short you serve.

The first key is to serve in such a way that he can't tee-off hard on your serve. By mixing up long, short, and half-long serves it will be very difficult for him to attack strong. Also, if you serve very low, heavy backspin short to the forehand, your opponent probably won't be able to produce much spin on the flip. If you serve to the backhand short, your opponent might be able to generate spin using the wrist – similar to Zhang Jike.

The second key is to learn how to attack the flip. If you merely block the flip, then your opponent will likely finish you off with a strong loop. If you are able to start your racket high, shorten your backswing, and loop with good control, then you will likely take the attack away from your opponent and he will usually block the next ball. Avoid blocking flips AND avoid hitting too hard against flips. Because the flip is so close to you, you don't have much time to adjust to the various speeds, spins, and trajectories. So, watch where he is flipping, adjust with your feet, start your hand high, and loop with control to a good location.

There is no reason to get frustrated trying to completely STOP your opponent from flipping your serve. Instead, serve in such a way that he cannot flip hard and BE PREPARED to attack his flip. A good example of how to attack flips can be seen in Dimitri Ovcharov's match against Zhang Jike at the 2014 World Championship.

Chapter 8: Mental Strength

Day 71
Proper Execution

If I asked you to walk on a three-foot wide plank of wood lying on the floor, could you do it?

What if I asked you to walk on a three-foot wide plank of wood that was extended across Niagara Falls, could you do it?

You would probably have confidence to do the first, but would not have confidence to do the second. What is different about the two tasks? …The consequences!

As soon as you begin thinking about the consequences, executing the shots becomes more difficult. Instead of focusing on losing ratings points or winning prize money, you should focus on executing your shots. Remember that you have trained your shots to perfection. Tournaments should not be very different from your practice. Just perform in the way that you have practiced without added pressure.

Day 72
Pre-game Routine

Before a match, it is vitally important that you prepare physically and mentally. Physically, you should prepare by jogging, stretching, and practicing 1-2 hours on the table. Mentally, you should prepare by strategizing, writing your thoughts, and relaxing.

You should first form your strategy by video analysis, especially if you know who your main opponents will be prior to the tournament. When watching the video, you should look for his strengths, weaknesses, and common game patterns. You should also study his serve, serve return, and end-game tendencies. In one column of the paper, write how your opponent wants to win points. In another column, write your strategy against him. The other way that you should strategize is by talking to others. Many times other coaches and players can tip you off on things that don't seem obvious.

Next, try to watch this opponent at the tournament and write some last-minute tips – usually three things that you must remember between every point. After writing these last-minute tips, practice before the match using the specific tactics that you plan to use against this opponent. You should also ask a training partner to serve similar serves as your opponent so you can practice against them.

Your final preparation is to relax. You might want to even go out in the hallway, stretch out, and clear your mind for ten minutes. After the final stage, continue to remind yourself that it is just a game, that you just need to play how you have practiced, that it will be fun, and that you love competitive matches!

Day 73
Post Game Routine

Table Tennis matches can be fairly emotional – regardless if you win or lose. For this reason, I would recommend using a post-game routine, which consists of relaxing, writing your thoughts, forgetting the previous match, and focusing on the next match.

The first essential aspect is to get away from the table and relax. It is important to take each match like a tournament. If you jump into the next match without a minute break, you will probably be less than 100% physically and mentally prepared.

The second essential aspect is to write your thoughts from the previous match. This should take less than one minute. Write 3-4 good strategies that you used and 3-4 things that you would do differently next time.

The third essential aspect is to forget the previous match. What? Forget it? I thought that I was supposed to write my thoughts? Yes, you did do that. Now forget it. Getting too high on a great victory or bumming-out too much on a bad loss will hinder your progress for the next match.

The final essential aspect is to focus on the next match. Go back through your pre-game routine, review your notes, and remember your strategy for your next opponent. Regardless of his/her level, take this next match like it is its own separate tournament. Relax, play your game, remember your strategy, be willing to adjust, and have fun!

Day 74
Throw a Curve Ball

You have heard the expression many times, "My boss threw me a curve ball," or "my day threw me a curve ball." The expression basically means, something happened that you didn't expect. In a close table tennis match, it is important to "throw a curve ball" at your opponent, something that he doesn't expect. At the same time, it is critical that you do something that you can reasonably achieve.

Here might be some good options for you:
- Serving from a different location
- Receiving in a different fashion
- Changing the pace on a loop or block
- Adding subtle amount of sidespin
- Playing slightly further back and allowing the ball to drop
- Playing slightly closer to the table and contacting the ball earlier

Here would be some poor options for you:
- Playing with the opposite hand
- Playing mind games with your opponent
- Playing a trick shot (behind the back or between the legs)

Many matches have been won or lost from a strategy change at 9-9 in the final game. Choose wisely what you hope to do and be willing to adjust if your opponent receives it easily. Throughout your practice sessions leading up to the tournament, try to spend at least 20-30 minutes per day training this "curve ball."

Day 75
Trouble, Trouble, Trouble

Some opponents like to cause controversy to break your concentration. This trouble-maker might cheat on the score, break the ball, complain about your serve, delay the game, or try to distract you in many other ways. So what should you do in this particular situation?

Stay Calm
If you get worked up over this cheater, he will have accomplished his goal. If you stay calm, you can keep your focus.

Get an Umpire
An umpire will deal with him so that you don't waste your energy arguing.

Remember Your Strategy
Instead of focusing on this trouble-maker, focus on your strategy. Focus on implementing your game plan and ball placement.

Character First
Regardless of how your opponent is acting, maintain composure and focus on showing good character. Two wrongs don't make a right.

Day 76
Guess or Not to Guess?

In table tennis, there are two aspects of anticipation. The first is to have a reasonable guess as to where your opponent will hit the next ball. The next aspect is watching his body position and racket angle and adjusting based on the direction of his swing.

Before serving, you should look at your opponent and try to think how he might return various serves. For example, this opponent (with very poor footwork) forehand loops well, forehand pushes well, backhand flips well, but can't backhand loop or forehand flip. From those quick observations, you can next decide what you are going to serve. If you serve long to the backhand, he will probably push or block, depending on your spin. If you serve short to the forehand, his only option is to push. If you serve short to the backhand, he could flip or push.

As you can see from the above examples, when serving, you should think about what your opponent can and cannot do. You should somewhat guess how he wants to receive based on his ready position, body language, and past history of receives. However, when serving, you should also be prepared to adjust in case he does the unexpected. These same principles apply to rallies. If you loop a forehand from your backhand side to your opponent's forehand, you need to adjust with your body and get ready for the crosscourt block. Still, your racket needs to be in front, you need to be on your toes, and you need to be watching your opponent's racket in-case he does something unexpected.

When receiving serve, you should NOT guess. You should be about one arm-length away from the table to prepare for the long serve. If the serve is short or half-long, move forward and receive the serve. If you guess what spin is coming, you will often be wrong. Watch your opponent's body position, toss, backswing, and contact point. Then adjust your swing based on the spin and bounce.

Anticipation is important. Sometimes after a serve or in a rally, it is okay to make an educated guess. Just remember not to fully commit until you see for sure where the ball is traveling. Also remember to continually adjust and re-adjust with your feet.

Day 77
Conviction

Most of my knowledge in table tennis comes from asking myself and others one main question…

"Why?"
- Why do you hold the racket like that?
- Why do you bend your knees?
- Why do you position your feet like that?
- Why do you lean forward?
- Why do you turn your body?
- Why do you start your racket in that position?
- Why do you turn your body?
- Why do you finish your stroke there?
- Why do you serve like that?
- Why do you want to hit that ball in that position?
- Why? Why? Why?

Now that I have a deeper conviction about my own personal game, it is easier to make improvements, form strategies, and teach others. So, today I challenge you to do this in your own game. Sit down and write out the "whys" about each part of your game – serve, serve return, footwork, loop, block, push, smash, flip, and all other parts. If you don't understand one part of your game, then ask another player or coach for some advice.

Let me walk you through one basic stroke (forehand push) by asking you a few simple questions...

- Why do you start your angle like that on your forehand push?
- Why is it important to maintain the same angle throughout the stroke?
- Why do you open your angle more if your opponent has more backspin?
- Why do you continue your stroke through the ball when pushing deep?
- Why do you step forward when pushing a short ball?
- Why do you step forward with your right foot ... why not the left?
- Why do you lean forward?
- Why do you hold your left hand in that position?
- Why do you start your racket in front of your body?
- Why do you step back after you push?
- Why do you push to that position on the table?

After answering many questions like these about each part of your game, I hope that you will play with more confidence and conviction. If there are changes that need to be made, seek help and make the necessary changes.

Day 78
The World-Class Mindset

Question: Samson, how can I improve my mental game?

Answer: Choose a level-headed, world-class player and copy him. When studying this elite athlete there are several things that you should be looking for.

Attitude
Throughout the training session, the elite athlete is picturing the tournament. He is picturing who he might be playing against, picturing what strategies he might use, and training to meet his goals. His mind is focused on training hard for winning. His mental focus is the same during a training session as it is during an important tournament. On the flip side, many American players view club night as a social time to just ping around, but then tragically put too much pressure on themselves during competitions.

Attitude During Warm-Up
When the elite athlete steps up to the table for his forehand/backhand warm-up prior to a match, he is confident, consistent, and plays control shots to get a good feel for the ball, lighting, table, and other playing conditions. On the flip side, many club players try to swing wildly and get very frustrated when they can't properly execute 5-6 consecutive forehands.

Attitude Between Points
The elite athlete isn't rushed. He takes plenty of time between points to focus. He also keeps his eyes in the court. He isn't looking at the spectators or seeing if a photographer is zoomed in for a cover photo. Even if he is nervous, he won't show it. Before each point, he goes through his "think circle" and completes his pre-point routine. On the flip side, many club players are too rushed between points and unable to think clearly point-by-point. They are also easily distracted by other matches, tournament announcements, coaches, spectators, photographers, their opponent, and many other things.

Reaction to Points Won
If the elite athlete wins a point, he sometimes expresses it outwardly, sometimes expresses it inwardly. He remembers what he did right and tries to repeat a similar strategy throughout the match. If a club player wins an awesome point, he sometimes celebrates so much that he isn't focused for the next point. Sometimes when a club player wins a point, he is still too critical, saying, "Bob, what are you thinking! Use your backhand? … or … Bob, why can't you be more aggressive?" Sometimes club members are even critical or insulting toward their opponents, perhaps saying, "Bob, you should be playing like this every point! This guy is easy!"

Reaction to Points Lost
When the elite athlete loses a point, he tries to contain his emotions. If he happens to lose control of his emotions, he will step away from the table, calm himself down, refocus, say something positive to himself, and then come back very focused for the next point. Even if he feels like hitting the table or breaking a barrier, he tries to contain himself because he realizes that any outward emotion will boost his opponent's confidence and ruin his own confidence. On the flip side, many club

players are so negative that they lose multiple points in a row out of frustration from a previous point. In table tennis, there are many runs in points; one player will often score 3-4 points, and then the other player will score 3-4 points. By minimizing the frustration and focusing on strategy, you should be able to minimize your opponent's runs.

Attitude Between Games
When an elite athlete wins or loses the first game, he remains composed. He isn't celebrating his win or grieving his loss. He keeps everything in perspective – knowing how to correct his flaws and knowing how to capitalize on his winning strategy. Between games, the club player is often very excited and already begins to calculate his new rating or he is depressed and begins to wonder what people will think about him if he loses. Instead of focusing on the strategy, the club member mistakenly focuses on the results of the match.

If you want to improve, then you need to start training like an elite athlete. The best way to begin is by THINKING like an elite athlete.

Day 79
You are a Loser

If you are a tournament player, shaking off a loss will be one of the biggest hurdles that you need to jump. This entire article can be summed up in one sentence...

Stop the excuses, admit you lost.

After admitting to yourself that you lost that match and it was your fault, you will then be able to clearly think why you lost and you will learn from your mistakes. If you continue to make excuses, then you won't change, you won't improve, and you will keep losing.

After losing in tournaments, here are some of the excuses that I have personally heard people say...

Quote #1: "Well, he was higher rated!"
Oh, so you are allowed to lose to him? During the match, were you fine with losing because he had a higher rating? What if you played the same player and he had a lower rating?

Quote #2: "Well, his family was there!"
Please remind me to bring my family to every tournament. I never realized that people let me win if my family is present! This is one of the worse excuses ever.

Quote #3: "Well, I didn't get a good warm-up!"
Ummm, whose fault is that? You should plan in advance to arrive 1-2 hours early with a training partner pre-arranged. You should practice for at least 20 min. and play at least one match prior to your first tournament match. If you aren't able to practice much, as least do plenty of stretching and jogging.

Quote #4: "Well, I just wasn't ON!"
Could you please be more specific? If one area of your game wasn't working, could you do something else? Could you slow down? Could you spin more? Could you focus on placement instead of power? Just because one aspect isn't up to par, doesn't mean that you need to shut down and quit!

Quote #5: "Well, his forehand loop was on fire!"
Was there any possible way to prevent or stop his forehand? What if you served short? What if you attacked first? What if you played to the wide backhand? What if you played to the extreme forehand?

Quote #6: "Well, he was cheating – he was serving from his fingers, not his palm!"
Just for starters, serving from the fingers doesn't give any advantage at all unless your opponent was spinning it from his fingers. Also, if you have a problem with it, politely ask your opponent to serve properly. If he persists, then graciously ask for an umpire.

Quote #7: "Well, he kept rushing me between points!"
Your opponent is not allowed to serve until you are ready. If the ball is on your side, walk slowly to retrieve the ball while thinking of your next strategy. If it is your serve, take your time. If it is your opponent's turn to serve, step back and take a breath before getting low in your ready position. If needed, use your timeout as well as your six-point towel breaks.

Quote #8: "Well, I couldn't get over the fact that his rating was so low; he is a sandbagger!"
His rating should not be a distraction. Remember that you are playing against an opponent, not against a rating. If you feel like this might possibly be a hindrance to your tournament, then avoid looking at your opponent's rating prior to the match. If you need to record the score then ask a coach or friend to do it for you.

Quote #9: "Well, I just didn't sleep much last night!"
Try to get extra rest in the previous 2-3 days prior to a tournament. If you still didn't get enough sleep, then eat some fruit prior to your match or drink some Gatorade. During the match, don't dwell on

what you can't change (like getting more sleep) but do dwell on what you can change (your game strategy).

Quote #10: "Well, I got really hungry during the match!"
Meal planning is a major part of tournament performance. At each lengthy break during a tournament, force yourself to eat a small meal. Between matches, have some healthy snacks to keep up your energy. At our tournaments here in Ohio, you will be fed both lunch and dinner. ☺

Quote #11: "Well, I didn't find out until after the match that he had anti-spin rubber!"
Before beginning any match, you should check your opponent's racket. Even if you have played against him in a previous tournament, you should still check. This is a really poor excuse.

Quote #12: "Well, I didn't know that I needed to win that match to advance from the group!"
Regardless if you would have advanced or not, you need to perform your best. Put out your best effort to win every last point. Putting more or less pressure on yourself by looking ahead at the results/consequences is a poor mental strategy.

Quote #13: "Well, he got too many nets and edges!"
Did you attempt to return them? You should do your best to return them, but still realize that nets and edges are only a small fraction of the points. Throughout that match, your opponent might have scored 45 points total. Out of those 45, how many did he actually score from nets and edges? Possibly 7-8 points. I realize that those two net-balls at 9-9 really put the nail in the coffin (I do have some sympathy), but there were other points that you lost during the match as well. What about that smash that you missed at 4-5 in the last game. Or what about those two backhand loops that you missed at 6-6 in the last game. What about the 18 serves that you misread the spin over the course of the five games? There were other mistakes. Don't blame the nets and edges for the loss.

Sorry, my reader. If I quoted you, I hope that you are not offended with my bluntness. Next time you lose a match … admit to yourself that you lost and do your ultimate best to improve for your next match!

Day 80
Dead Time

The average match in table tennis takes about 20 minutes. Out of the 20 minutes, about five minutes total is spent on rallies. The other 15 minutes is spent picking up the ball, preparing for the serve, taking towel breaks, taking timeouts, and getting coaching advice. So, here is the question that I would like for you to consider…

If only 25% of the match time is spent playing points, then why do we spend 99.9% of our effort on that portion of the game and we spend about 0.1% of our effort on the dead time???

We must remember that the time between points, the time picking up balls, and the towel-off breaks have a huge impact on what happens DURING the point. Wrong thoughts lead to wrong playing.

Here are some wrong thoughts…

Prior to the match
If I lose this match, I'll lose 13 points. If I win this match, I'll gain 6 points. I better not lose or I'll drop below 1800.

Beginning of the match
I hate playing against long pips. Those pips should be outlawed. I bet his pips are illegal.

After developing a great lead in the first game
Wow, this match is much easier than I thought. Maybe I should start practicing some of those backhand serves for the next opponent. Let's experiment a little.

After losing the first game
This is just not my day. Bob (playing on the next table) is too loud. I hate playing next to his table. Why isn't the food here yet I'm getting hungry? My cousin said that he would be here, he should be clapping for me. It's just not my day. I shouldn't have come to this tournament.

Here are some right thoughts...

Prior to the match
Ok, I have analyzed my opponent's game and I know his strengths and weaknesses. I'm going to focus on attacking these two weak point. I must remember to adjust as the match progresses.

Beginning of the match
Ok, now I must remember my strategy and keep my eyes in the court. I must remember to keep my focus.

After developing a great lead in the first game
Yes, my strategy is working. I need to continue using the strategy that is working and be aware of my mistakes so that I can adjust.

After losing the first game
Ok, now I have a very good feel of what is working and what isn't working. I'm now ready to re-adjust my strategy and start well in the second game. If I start off losing, I'll call timeout early. I must remember to take my time between points so that I can think clearly.

Day 81
Can You Sense the Future?

If you look, listen, and feel between points, you can have an idea of what your opponent might possibly do in the next rally.

Look
After the point has finished, look at your opponent. Without knowing it, he might be frantically waving his arms, demonstrating what he should have done or demonstrating what he wants to do. For example, you just surprised him with a deep serve to his middle (he used a backhand push). Disgustedly, he does a shadow stroke showing that he wants to use his forehand loop. Knowing that he wants to use his forehand loop on the next serve return, should give you (as the server) a much better idea of what to serve and what to expect from him as the receiver.

Listen
After the point has finished, listen for your opponent's mumbling response. Many players mumble under their breath without knowing it. Some opponents will do it on purpose to mess you up, but most of your opponents do it unknowingly because they are in the habit of doing it. For example, if you just served heavy backspin short to your

opponent's backhand and he flipped it into the bottom of the net, you might hear him mumble, "C'mon, Billy, just push the ball!" So at that moment, you need to decide if Billy said that for you to hear, or did Billy say it to himself. If Billy said that to himself, then he will probably make a passive return next.

Feel
Before serving, look at your opponent. From the look on his face, to the tension in his muscles, to his right/left position at the table, to his distance away from the table, to his stance, to his racket height, to his grip, you should be able to tell if he wants to receive the serve with his backhand or forehand and whether he wants to receive aggressively with a flip or loop or passively with a push or chop. If you spend enough time studying various opponents, you will learn to get a feel of what they might possibly do.

You might only have about 8-10 seconds between each point, so use this time wisely to analyze the last point, clear your mind, build your confidence, LOOK & LISTEN & FEEL, and then strategize for the next point.

Day 82
Be the Front Runner

In table tennis, try your best to build an early lead in points, try your best to win the first game, and try your best to win the match 3-0.

One of my students recently lost to a player who had an amazing forehand and a terrible backhand. This opponent's forehand was at least 1900-level and his backhand was around 800-1000 level. After losing, I asked my student why he played so many balls to the forehand. He responded by saying, "Well, I didn't want my opponent to know that I knew his weak point." What a terrible way to lose a match.

If your opponent has an obvious weak point, play to the weak point. The most devastating thing for your opponent is for him to feel trapped, for him to feel vulnerable that you have found his weak point and continue to win points against it.

If the opponent in the above situation is smart, he will probably try to step around and play his forehand from the backhand side. At this point, you might need to THEN expose the wide forehand, then go back to the backhand. If your opponent doesn't cover for his weak point, keep playing to it. Don't let him off the hook!

An early lead is also important because it puts more pressure on your opponent. As you continue to win points, you should feel more relaxed while still being able to think clearly and strategizing. Also, a "lucky-shot" such as a mis-hit or a net or an edge isn't as devastating at 10-4. If the score is 7-7 and he scores a couple lucky shots, you might be in trouble. If you build that early lead in points or an early lead in games, it won't hurt you as much.

Take your time between points, keep strategizing, use your timeout early, use your strong weapons, pick on your opponent's weak points, and do everything possible to get that early lead!

Day 83
The Mental Timeout

In table tennis, each player has one timeout per match lasting up to 60 seconds. Experienced tournament players are aware of this and use it at the appropriate time. However, many players don't use their mental timeouts. During a match, a player is allowed to take a brief towel-off break every six points. So if the score is 5-1 or 10-8 or 12-12, the player can take a towel-off break. I call it my "mental timeout" – the time that I can step back from the table for a few seconds, clear my mind, encourage myself, consider what I have been doing right or wrong, and form new strategies.

So on a six-point break, should you take your mental timeout (towel-off break)? Below I have listed some situations where you SHOULD take your mental timeout:

1. You should take your mental timeout if you are tired or if you need to rest or dry off.

2. You should take your mental timeout if you are losing. You should consider how to correct your mistakes, how to expose your opponent's weak points, and how to use your strengths.

3. You should take your mental timeout if you are winning but your opponent scored the last couple points. Let's say that you were winning 10-5. Your opponent comes back to 10-8. You now need a quick mental timeout to re-assess the situation, focus, and play your best.

4. You should take your mental timeout if you don't have a good game plan. You aren't sure what to serve or you aren't sure what strategies to implement. Then, give yourself a brief moment to think clearly and form a quick strategy.

Many players are aware of the towel-off break, but few players use it effectively. Use it in practice, use it at the club, and use it in tournaments. Table tennis is about 50% physical and 50% mental. Many average players make mistakes over and over again. Many professional players make mistakes – however, they are able to re-assess the situation, learn from their mistakes, and adjust accordingly.

Chapter 9: Health

Day 84
Eat Up the Competition

Most professional athletes have very strict diets. They feast for breakfast, eating healthy food with good carbohydrates, eat normal for lunch, and eat a light dinner.

Why do they eat so much early in the day? They eat large amounts of food to fuel their workouts. Without the proper carbohydrate intake, they cannot give 100% to practice because they run out of energy after 1-2 hours. The large intake of food in the morning is what fuels their workouts.

Why do they eat a normal size lunch? Because they ate so much food earlier in the day, they can just re-fuel for lunch. Without a good breakfast, they would be at a deficit for the rest of the day.

Why do they eat light before going to bed? At night, they don't need a large meal for sleeping.

Throughout the day, these athletes also drink plenty of fluids. On training days, most pro athletes drink about 8-10 quarts of water. On resting days, they drink about 4-5 quarts of water. Dehydration is one of the main reasons that table tennis players become so fatigued and lose energy during training and tournaments.

Snacking is another great way to maintain energy. Proper meal planning and having healthy snacks available is one of the best ways to avoid grabbing chips from the vending machine or a Big Mac meal from the drive through. Fuel your workout properly and you will be able to maintain a healthy weight while giving your best through every training session.

Day 85
Sleep Positioning

Did you know that you can improve your forehand while sleeping? Most table tennis players are very one-sided. From the constant body rotation with their forehand loops, most players have very flexible cores when rotating to the right (for right-handed players). However, these same players are not very flexible when rotating to the left. This is one of the reasons that many elite table tennis athletes have to constantly battle against lower back pain.

I personally have had many back problems. Recently, I was talking with my physical therapist and he made a recommendation. He recommended that I sleep on my right side. Sleeping on my right side really did balance out the lack of range of motion in that direction. Most people (like myself) when sleeping on their right side cross their left leg over so that they are rotated a bit like a lefty's forehand loop backswing position. In this position, it is able to balance out the lack of movement in that direction.

It might sound crazy to think that you can improve your table tennis game while you sleep ... and you might not believe me ... but hey, give it a try! Sleeping on my right side has helped my back tremendously. I plan to continue sleeping on my right side so that I can have better balance between right and left side flexibility.

Day 86
Table Tennis Fuel

It is 2pm on a Saturday afternoon. You are just about to leave for the table tennis club and practice hard from 3-6pm. You need some extra energy to fuel your training session. What should you get? A triple-thick chocolate milkshake from McDonalds? Three candy bars from Wal-Mart? A Java Monster from Speedway? I would recommend a high-energy fruit smoothie.

Here is my newest mixture that I have recently been enjoyed over the past 1-2 months...

- 1 cup of ice
- 1 cup of fresh mango (cut up)
- ½ cup of fresh strawberries
- ½ cup of strawberry Greek yogurt
- ½ cup of apple juice
- ½ cup of milk

Blended together it makes two servings of the most amazing smoothie I have ever drank. If you prefer the smoothie to be slightly thicker, then add a bit less apple juice and milk. If you don't have fresh mangos and strawberries, you can also use frozen ones; in that case, do not add ice with it.

Although it is difficult to eat a full meal just prior to your matches, it is very easy to drink a smoothie 20-30 minutes before your first match; which will give you energy for a couple hours.

Day 87
Diets

Today, I'm going to briefly mention some basic nutrition rules that I have learned and try diligently to practice and encourage my students to practice as well.

Rule #1: Diets Don't Work
Many of my friends have gone on 30-day or 60-day diets. After losing 20 pounds from practically starving themselves, they are so excited, but their bodies are in shock. So, when they return to their normal eating, their bodies hold on to the fat. They lose 20 pounds but end up gaining 30 pounds. Instead of going on a diet this year, consider a permanent life change. Seriously consider changing your eating habits for life!

Rule #2: Cheating Doesn't Finish the Diet
Sometimes, one of my friends will cheat on his diet by eating an extremely unhealthy meal. After that, he quits his diet because he wrecked it. That is terrible. Instead of straying away, just return to it the next day or the next week.

Rule #3: Be Selective
Starving yourself for a good length of time isn't healthy. Instead of starving, eat normal HEALTHY meals. Be selective on what you buy at the grocery store and what you order at the restaurant.

Rule #4: Consider the Switch
A few years ago, I made the switch to whole grains – oatmeal instead of cereal, 100% whole wheat bread instead of white bread, brown rice instead of white rice, whole grain pasta instead of normal pasta. When I began eating more whole grains, my energy lasted longer and I didn't have any stomach problems. It was also easier for me to stay leaner.

Rule #5: Snacking
Light snacking can be okay if it is done in moderation. Some healthy snacks that I would recommend would include bananas, celery and peanut butter, nuts, carrot sticks, or a fruit smoothie.

Rule #6: Drinks
Some Americans drink over 2000 calories per day. These are simple sugars that don't last long and will leave you hungry in a short period of time. Consider drinking only water throughout the day. Many people who have switched to drinking only water have easily lost ten pounds from making the change. I try to drink around 6-8 quarts per day. If you aren't working out much, I would recommend about four quarts. If you are training hard, you should try to drink 8 quarts per day. Also, many food cravings can be caused by dehydration.

Day 88
Table Tennis Breakfast

From Asia to Africa to Europe, there are thousands of professional table tennis athletes who are aspiring to be the next World Champion. One of the key elements to reaching the top is consistent training six hours per day. Most top players wake up, eat breakfast, train three hours, eat lunch, rest, then train three more hours in the late afternoon. Breakfast is the most important meal of the day to fuel an intense early morning session.

Uncooked oatmeal is the key. Here are the ingredients for one serving:
- 1 cup of uncooked rolled oats
- ¼ cup of sliced almonds
- ¼ cup of raisins or ½ cup of fresh fruit
- 1 cup of milk

Mix them all together in a bowl. Preparation time is one minute.

Here are the nutrition facts:
- Calories 730
- Carbs 104 grams
- Protein 25 grams
- Fiber 14 grams

Every morning, I eat two servings of The Table Tennis Breakfast, and it gives me the right balance of healthy carbs and protein to fuel an intense training session.

Before I discovered The Table Tennis Breakfast, I used to eat three bowls of cereal or prepackaged oatmeal, two pieces of fruit, and two bagels. This breakfast would give me energy for approximately two hours. Cooked, pre-packaged oatmeal only offers about 1/3 cup of oats but expands when it is heated. It appears to fill the bowl, but is digested in less than half the time. Additionally, prepackaged oatmeal is loaded with unnecessary sugars and preservatives.

I challenge you to try it for one week – The Table Tennis Breakfast! You will feel energized and will avoid morning cravings for at least four hours. This breakfast is the key for anyone aspiring to move to the next level.

Chapter 10: Equipment

Day 89
Carbon Blades Compared to Wood Blades

Generally, carbon blades are faster and more suitable for the advanced player. For a beginner, it is best to choose a very slow, controlled wood blade. This will allow the player to develop solid strokes because the ball has more dwell-time on the racket. A faster blade is better for an attacking player who contacts the ball at the top of the bounce. A controlled blade is better for a defensive or all-around player who plays from many different distances from the table.

Wood blades have more feel and vibration than carbon blades. As a beginner, it is important to "feel" the ball. For this reason, I would suggest using an all-wood blade for the first three years. After a player has excellent strokes and feeling, it would be advisable to possibly move up to a carbon blade for added power. At the elite level, players who mainly use power to win points generally play with carbon blades for a hard feel. Elite players who use touch to win points generally play with all-wood blades for a much softer feel.

Carbon blades have a larger sweet-spot due to the re-inforced layers and harder feeling of the blade. This will give slightly more room for error if the player doesn't contact the ball in the center of the racket.

The final factor to consider is the cost. Most wood blades cost from $40-$100. Most carbon blades cost from $60-$200. If a player uses the racket for at least one year, paying the extra money is possibly worth it. The racket will last for 5-10 years.

    A. Carbon blades are generally faster (but not always)
    B. Carbon blades have less vibration and a harder feel
    C. Carbon blades have a larger sweet-spot
    D. Carbon blades cost more

Day 90
Sponge Thickness

What is the effect of sponge thickness? Is it the same for anti/long pips rubber as for offensive rubber? Thicker sponge gives more of a trampoline effect, producing more speed and spin. Most offensive players use sponge that is at least 2.0mm. Thinner sponge gives more control and feels harder because the ball sinks deeper to the wood. Many defensive players use sponge that is 1.0-2.0mm.

Another factor to consider is the weight. For senior citizens, kids, and beginners, I recommend a light racket. Having 1.0-2.0mm sponge will help keep the racket light.

Anti/long pips rubbers are not grippy and therefore give spin reversal. By having sponge, the anti/long pips will grip the ball more and give less reversal. For the nastiest block with spin reversal, I suggest to use no sponge or very thin sponge. For the mid to long distance chopper, I suggest to use 1.5mm sponge to give more speed to the ball. From fifteen feet away from the table, the racket must have some speed to carry the ball back to the table. Although it will have less reversal, it will be able to produce more spin on its own and will be more consistent from that distance.

Thicker sponge:
1. Is faster
2. Is spinnier
3. Has less control
4. Is heavier
5. Gives less reversal on anti/long pips
6. Gives more of its own spin on anti/long pips

Day 91
Sponge Hardness/Density

The hardness/density affects how deep the ball sinks into the sponge. Softer sponge will have more dwell time and allow the ball to sink deeper, giving the ball a higher arc. Most loopers and those focusing on spinny shots and more arc prefer soft sponge. Softer sponge is lighter in weight and makes it easier to create spin on slower shots: slow loops against backspin, chop, and push. Harder sponge has less dwell time and does not allow the ball to sink deep into the sponge. Many aggressive counterlooping players like harder sponge because there is more potential for power and spin from mid-distance. Although harder sponge is heavier, one must also consider the sponge thickness when gauging the weight.

Most rubbers have two versions, a soft one and a hard one. This doesn't mean that the hard is extremely hard or the soft is extremely soft. It just means that one is softer than the other. Before purchasing a rubber, consult the equipment catalog review on each rubber.

Day 92
Light Blade vs Heavy Blade Comparison

The weight difference is due to several factors: the materials used, the head size, the number of plies, and the handle type. If the blade has a hollow handle, it will be more top heavy. If the blade has a solid handle, it will be more equally balanced from top to bottom.

Generally, close-to-the-table players use light blades, less than 70-90 grams. A light blade provides more racket speed and quickness for a good backhand/forehand transition. Choppers and lobbers use heavier blades, 90-100 grams. Because the distance player has more time to react to the ball, a heavy blade will provide more stability and consistency away from the table.

Children under thirteen years old, elderly beginners, and anyone with limited strength should use a racket that is 70-80 grams. This will allow them to have good racket speed and develop proper strokes without battling fatigue.

Day 93
Large Head vs Small Head Comparison

Generally, larger head blades are heavier and smaller head blades are lighter. Close-to-the-table attackers often use small blades because they are easy to maneuver for serve, serve return, and over the table pushes and attacks. Also, when swinging a small head blade, there will be less wind-resistance. Distance choppers and lobbers often use larger blades because they have a better chance of hitting the ball, and quick maneuvering isn't an issue.

Another factor to consider is the amount of rubber that it takes to cover the racket. Smaller head blades will be lighter because they require less rubber to cover the surface. Large head blades will be much heavier and become slightly top heavy with the added weight near the end of the racket.

Day 94
Lifetime of the Rubber

Inverted rubber lasts about 60 hours for the advanced club player. If the player uses it every day for two hours, it should be changed once per month. If he uses it twice per week for two hours, it should be changed every four months. Cleaning the rubber after each every practice session and sealing it with adhesive rubber protection sheets is the best way to ensure the full 60 hours of use.

Anti-spin rubber usually lasts for 2-5 years. With no friction, the rubber actually becomes better with age. The only way for the anti rubber to wear out is for the sponge to degrade. Check to ensure that the rubber bounces equally on all parts of the blade. Pips rubber usually lasts about 100-150 hours. The rubber is worn-out when the pips begin to break or the sponge degrades, giving it an inconsistent bounce.

Day 95
Got Junk?

Today, I'm going to classify all table tennis rubbers into one of three basic categories.

Grippy Inverted Rubbers
What you see is what you get. If your opponent strokes the ball with a topspin stroke, the ball will be topspin to some degree or another. Same principle applies to backspin or sidespin.

Recreational Rubbers, Short Pips, and Long Pips with Grip
What you see is not what you get. Even though your opponent might appear to be spinning the ball, the ball will usually have little spin.

Anti-spin Rubbers and Long-Pips without Friction
What you see is not what you get. If you impart light spin on the ball, when your opponent returns the ball (even if it appears that he is spinning) the ball will be without spin. If you impart very heavy spin on the ball, then your opponent's ball with have some spin coming back to you. If you impart very heavy backspin, then the ball with have some topspin coming back. If you impart very heavy topspin, then the ball with have some backspin coming back. The trouble that most players encounter is that they impart very little spin on the ball, then are surprised when the pips or anti return comes back without spin. The main point that you must remember is that anti and pips don't create spin, they just return the ball with your spin.

Day 96
Your Backup Racket

Disaster might strike at your next tournament...

- You might accidentally drop your racket and break it during a match.
You might accidentally damage your rubber on the corner of the table.
- You might have rubber that is somehow illegal.
- Your racket might get stolen.
-

    Unfortunately, these are problems that sometimes come up. Fortunately, most players are prepared enough to have a backup racket; HOWEVER, most player don't like their backup racket as much as their first racket. Many players have backup rackets that are different from their primary racket.

    I recommend having a backup racket that is identical in every aspect – including age of the blade and age of the rubber. Practice with both your primary racket and your backup racket prior to your next tournament. Make sure that both rackets are exactly identical in every aspect. Fall in love with your backup racket. When disaster strikes and you cannot use your primary racket, pull out your backup (with a smile) and keep your focus on your performance.

Chapter 11:
Your Future

Day 97
Thinking Ahead

This year, set some high goals in table tennis and work consistently to reach these goals. Look ahead to the competition 200 rating points ahead of you, and think about your previous matches against them in tournaments. What shots worked? What shots didn't work? Do you need to alter your strategy?

Being in Ohio, I play against many lower-rated players. There are strategies and serves that I can use against them that might not be effective against stronger players. I need to train for the next level by thinking about the particular strategies that will work against Damien Provost, Timothy Wang, Wang Zhen, and others. If I'm going to reach the next level, I need to start thinking, strategizing, and training at the next level. The same is true for you, my reader.

I want you to take out a pen and paper and spend about 10 minutes writing some notes. When you play against players who are 200 points higher than you at tournaments…

- Which serves worked?
- Which serves didn't work?
- Which serve returns worked?
- Which serve returns didn't work?
- Which offensive strokes worked?
- Which offensive strokes didn't work?
- Which defensive strokes worked?
- Which defensive strokes didn't work?

When you are competing against a lower player, sometimes your long, spinny serves will win the point outright. You might even be able to win 5-6 points each game from just your serve! However, when playing against a higher-level opponent, he might easily return ALL of your serves with strong loops. For this reason, choose the serve that best sets up your game (possibly a low, short serve).

When you are competing against a lower player, sometimes blocking one ball to the backhand will cause your opponent to miss outright. However, when playing against a higher-level opponent, he might return ALL of your blocks. For this reason, block the first ball with good placement, and then look to counterloop the next ball.

When you are competing against a lower player, sometimes smashing the ball to the forehand with full power will cause your opponent to miss outright. However, when playing against a higher-level opponent, he might step back from the table and fish it back to the table. For this reason, look to focus on placement with your smash, not just power. Also, you must be prepared to smash multiple balls. It might even take 5-10 well-placed smashes in order to finish off a good lobber.

When you are competing against a lower player, sometimes pushing deep and heavy will cause him to miss outright. However, when playing against a higher-level opponent, he might be able to loop your heavy push. For this reason, be ready to block his strong loop; or, better yet, find ways to attack first by pushing short or flipping.

When you are competing against a lower player, sometimes using a sharp angle will cause your opponent to miss outright. However, when playing against a higher-level opponent, he may use your sharp-angled shot against you by hitting an even wider angle. For this reason, learn to better anticipate the crosscourt ball. Also consider other placement variations like playing against his elbow – the transition point between forehand and backhand.

As you work toward reaching your goals this year, start thinking ahead to the higher competition. Even when playing against lower players at the club, play your new strategy. Playing at an elite level starts with thinking at an elite level.

Day 98
The Guinea Pig

Guinea pigs used for experiments usually don't last too long – many of them die. Do you feel like the guinea pig at the club? Is your game dying from too many experiments?

Throughout my playing career many people have personally given me advice about my game – I hear it from friends, strangers, relatives, practice partners, coaches, club members, and opponents in tournaments. Maybe you are in the same situation. Maybe you receive a lot of advice from others and sometimes feel like the guinea pig. Maybe you feel like people are experimenting with new ideas by telling you to do this and that when they themselves have never understood or used that particular skill.

The next time someone gives you advice, here is the thought process that you need to have:

1. First, be polite and thank the player for the tip.

2. Consider, is it appropriate to think about this change right now? If you are in the middle of a tournament, then you shouldn't be making major changes. If it is appropriate to think about making the change, then follow the next steps.

3. Ask the player if he can demonstrate his recommendation or if he knows of a player that you can watch who can demonstrate it.

4. Ask the player why he recommends the change and if the change would be something that would change your entire game (for possibly big results) or would it be a subtle change that would enhance your game (with the results perhaps a bit less obvious at first).

5. Once you have been convinced the change is needed, and have spent a significant amount of time visualizing the change, it is time to put in the work for making the change, through shadow stroking, robot training, simple drills, game-like drills, practice matches, and tournaments.

Maybe you feel like a guinea pig because people are always recommending new things for your game. It can be a bit depressing. However, once you are able to process the information correctly, then you can decide for yourself if this change would be helpful or not. But remember, always be kind and courteous so that others will be more willing to help you!

Day 99
Try Something New!

Each year, you should take about two weeks and try to experiment with some new skills in your table tennis game. During this time, instead of focusing on matches, focus on practice. Try to play every day with a robot or training partner. Here are some possible new things to try...

Distance
Instead of playing only one distance, try playing slightly closer to the table or slightly further back from the table.

Spin
Instead of looping with the same spin, try to add slightly more or less spin to give your loops more variation.

Serve
Instead of perfecting your current serve, try some new serves like backhand or hook or reverse pendulum or tomahawk.

Serve Return
Instead of returning short serves with a push, try to develop a consistent flip with good placement.

Sidespin
Instead of hitting your normal blocks, loops, and pushes, try adding a bit of sidespin as a tricky variation.

Defense
Instead of trying to attack every ball, allow your opponent to attack sometimes while you practice your chopping, passive blocking, active blocking, and counterloop.

Footwork
Instead of continually working on your basic footwork, try some advance moves, such as in-and-out or a crossover step.

Angles
Instead of merely hitting to your opponent's forehand and backhand, try hitting wider to see if you can widen the angles.

The possibilities are endless. After your two weeks of experimenting, write out a list of 2-3 things that you feel are vital for your improvement. Spend the next 12 months working hard to improve these areas. Ask advice from coaches and other club members. Record your practice sessions and games while being persistent to make the changes.

Day 100
Steps to Perfection

Learning a new skill in table tennis takes time. Some skills take about a month to develop, but most take about 2-3 years to fully master. During your 100-day journey, you have learned many skills. You are probably anxious to know when you will master these skills. So, today you will learn the steps to perfection. It is vitally important to go step-by-step, even if it takes a long time. You can apply this theory to any stroke; however, I'm going to use the backhand loop against block as an illustration.

Step 1: Understanding the Need
You have a great forehand loop. You are developing footwork in order to use your forehand as much as possible while still maintaining balance and control. However, you aren't able to cover the extreme angles and often get stuck blocking or counterdriving with your backhand. You also aren't able to attack strong against a hard, low block. You clearly understand that a backhand loop against topspin is vital to your game, and are willing to work hard to get this new weapon. Again, this thinking can be applied to any new skill, not just the backhand loop. The backhand loop is merely used for illustration purposes in these steps.

Step 2: Visualization
Next, you need to be able to visualize it in your mind. Start by watching some Youtube videos of the world's top players performing this stroke; if possible, watch the slow-motion version. Also, try to watch other club members, elite players at tournament, and especially some top coaches. This stage should take less than one week.

Step 3: Shadow Strokes
Stand in front of a large mirror. Holding your racket, perform about

100 strokes per day, trying your best to remember all the elements that you saw during your visualization – stance, foot positioning, shoulder, arm, wrist, racket angle, timing, backswing, contact point, follow through, and other aspects. Occasionally, pause and review the Youtube video over and over again for deeper visualization. This stage should take about a couple weeks.

Step 4: Hit the Ball
It is now time to give your new stroke a try! Using your table tennis robot, have the balls shoot slow topspin to your backhand court. You should be recording your backhand loop throughout the practice. Every 30 seconds, turn off the robot and quickly review the video. If you don't have access to a table tennis robot, ask a friend or club member to block slowly and consistently to your backhand. The goal is to get 20 consecutive backhand loops on the table. This might be the hardest stage and will likely take a few months to perfect.

Step 5: Changing Speeds
There are two aspects to this stage. The first is to adjust your own speed. You should be able to consistently loop slightly harder or softer while still maintaining consistency and spin. By giving variation in your game, you will be able to keep your opponent off balance. The second aspect is adjusting your opponent's speed. Have your training partner or robot hit the ball sometimes faster and sometimes slower to your backhand. When the fast ball comes, shorten your stroke while spinning through the ball. When the slow ball comes, lengthen your swing. Develop an adjustable stroke that will allow you to perform well against any style – regardless of the quick or slow timing. This stage will probably take about one month to somewhat develop and a lifetime of training to perfect. This stage needs to be repeated over and over again, even for professional players.

Step 6: Changing Distances
In table tennis, most players have a preferred distance that they like to play – near the table, mid-distance, or far from the table. However, in matches, it isn't always possible to stay at that exact distance. For this reason, it is good to learn to play all three distances and be able to smoothly move from distance to distance within the same rally. If you are closer to the table, shorten your stroke. If you are farther from the

table, lengthen your stroke. This stage will probably take about a couple of weeks.

Step 7: Combining Strokes
After you have perfected your new skill through the steps previously mentioned, it is time to move to the next stage – combining the strokes. By selecting drill #46, the Newgy Robot will shoot one ball to your backhand and one ball to your forehand. See if you can be consistent while moving into position and linking the shots together. This stage will probably take about one month.

Step 8: Semi-Systematic Drills
This stage is very similar to the last one, however, now there is a random factor to the drill. Using your Newgy 2050 robot, select drill #27. This drill will give you 1-3 balls to the backhand, and then surprise you with a ball to your wide forehand. Just like in a game, it is important to watch the approaching ball, then quickly transition to watching your opponent's racket or the robot's head. There are dozens of drills like this one. Semi-systematic means that the balls hit the table in a systematic pattern and sometimes give you a surprise. Other examples of semi-systematic drills include:
- 1 ball to the middle, then 1 ball to either corner
- 1 ball to the forehand, 1 ball to the backhand, and 2 balls random
- 1 or 2 balls to the forehand then 1 or 2 balls to the backhand

You will probably be using drills like these throughout your entire playing career. These drills are fun, challenging, and very game-like.

Step 9: Random
Random drills are very similar to semi-systematic, except they are much harder. During a random drill, the robot or training partner can hit the balls anywhere on the table or anywhere in a specified zone for any number of balls. You must be very focused and very flexible to adjust. I personally like to do random drills as the bulk of my training.

Step 10: Game Situation
Now that you have completed all the previous steps, you are now equipped to use your new skill in a game situation. Have your training

partner or robot start with a serve; you should attack the serve and then begin using your backhand loop in the drill. If you are performing the drills with a training partner, there are a variety of ways to start a game situation drill. You can serve and ask him to flip or push; or he can serve and you attack. Either way, the drill should work into a systematic, semi-systematic, or random drill. Before going to the club, you should be able to comfortably perform game-situation drills.

Step 11: Club
Here lies one of the main obstacles in perfecting a new skill – losing! At the expense of possibly losing a match, many players don't want to use their new stroke. First, you must realize that it is okay to lose to someone that you have beaten for the past two years. It is okay. Don't worry what other players might say. Next, think long-term. By thinking long-term, you will be able to keep temporary winning and losing in perspective. It is okay to lose today to Bob, because you will be beating everyone within 2-3 years. Tell yourself, "Tonight, I'm going to sacrifice present pleasures (possibly winning now) for future benefits (dominating later)!"

Step 12: Tournament
Playing tournaments is similar to playing club matches. Continue to remind yourself to do your best, be brave, do the right thing, apply your new skill, perform well, and let winning take care of itself. Be flexible and ready to adjust to a variety of playing styles. Take your time between points and encourage yourself. Your approach to a tournament should be no different than your approach to a club match.

Step 13: An Important Point
You have now been using your new skill successfully throughout the easy matches of the day. Now you are in the final of your event and the score is 9-9 in the last game. The entire tournament has stopped to watch this point. In this moment, it is all mental. You have proved to yourself through months of hard step-by-step training that you have mastered the skill and you are ready...

What are you going to do?
The choice is yours.

Glossary

American grip—See Seemiller grip.

Antispin—An inverted rubber sheet that is very slick so that spin does not take on it. It usually has a very dead sponge underneath. It is mostly used for defensive shots. Also known as "anti."

Backhand—A shot normally done with the racket to the left of the elbow for a right-hander, to the right for a left-hander.

Backspin—A type of spin used mostly on defensive shots. When you chop the ball, you produce backspin. The bottom of the ball will move away from you. The backspin pulls the ball up, while gravity pulls it down, so the ball tends to travel in a line. It is also called underspin or chop.

Banana flip (or flick)—A wristy backhand return of a short ball that's sort of a mini-loop, with topspin and sidespin, with racket moving from right to left (for a righty). Against a sidespin serve, you would mostly do this when you can go with the spin, i.e. against a forehand sidespin-type serve between two righties. The path the racket goes through is roughly like a banana.

Blade—The racket without covering.

Block—A quick, off the bounce return of an aggressive drive done by holding the racket in the ball's path.

Blocker—A style of play where blocking is the primary shot.

Chop—A defensive return of a drive with backspin, usually done from well away from the table. It is also sometimes used as another name for backspin.

Chop-block—A block against topspin where the racket is chopped down at contact to create backspin.

Chopper—A style of play where chopping is the primary shot. (See Chop.)

Closed racket—If the racket's hitting surface is aimed downward, with the top edge leaning away from you, it is closed.

Conventional penhold backhand—The way most penholders used to hit their backhands, using the same side of the racket as their forehands, and mostly blocking. This means less weakness in the middle and a better block, but limits the backhand attack.

Corkscrewspin—a type of spin that makes the ball jump sideways when it hits the table, most often done off a high-toss serve.

Counter-drive—A drive made against a drive. Some players specialize in counter-driving. Also known as counter-hitting.

Counter-hitter—See counter-drive.

Counter-loop—To loop against a loop.

Counter-smash—To smash against a smash.

Crosscourt—A ball that is hit diagonally from corner to corner.

Crossover—A style of footwork that require you to cross your feet. It is used to cover the wide forehand.

Dead—A ball with no spin.

Deep—A ball that will not bounce twice on the opponent's side of the table if given the chance.

Default—Getting disqualified from a match.

Double bounce—A ball that hits the same side of the table twice. The person on that side loses the point.

Down-the-line—A ball that is hit along the side of the table, parallel to the sidelines.

Drive—An aggressive topspin shot done forehand or backhand, but without as much topspin as a loop. Some players call an aggressive loop a "loop drive."

Drop shot—Putting the ball so short that the opponent has trouble reaching the ball. It is usually done when the opponent is away from the table. Given the chance, the ball would normally bounce twice on the table.

Fishing—A defensive topspin return from off the table, with the ball often returned a few feet or more above the net, but not as high as a lob.

Flat drive—A drive where the ball hits the racket almost straight on, putting little topspin on the ball.

Flick—See Flip.

Flip—An aggressive topspin attack of a short ball. In Europe it is called a flick.

Forehand—A shot normally done with the racket to the right of the elbow for a right-hander, to the left for a left-hander.

Free hand—The hand not holding the racket.

Half-long serve—A serve where, given the chance, the second bounce would be near the end line, making it difficult to loop. There are varying definitions for this. Some say the second bounce of a half-long serve always goes just off the end, so the end line gets in the way if the opponent tries to loop. Others say that the second bounce should always be just short of the end, so the serve is as deep as possible while still being short enough that it can't normally be looped. Others say that these are both half-long as long as the second bounce is near the end line. It is also called a "tweeny serve."

Handicap events—An event in a tournament where points are spotted to make the match even.

Hard rubber—A type of racket covering with pips out rubber but no sponge underneath. It was the most common covering for many years until the development of sponge rubber. Also called pimpled rubber.

Hardbat—A racket covered with hard rubber. Hardbat was the primary rackets used from the 1930s until the 1950s.

Heavy—A ball with a lot of spin, usually backspin.

Heavy no-spin—A no-spin shot, usually the serve, with a lot of motion to fake spin.

High-toss serve—A serve where the ball is thrown high into the air. This increases both spin and deception but is hard to control.

Hitter—A style of play where hitting is the primary shot.

Hook loop—a sidespin loop where a forehand loop breaks left (for a righty), or (less common) a righty's backhand loop breaks right (also for a righty).

Hyperbolic serve—An extremely fast serve with extreme topspin, often done with a forehand motion, but with contact made with the backhand side of the racket (by aiming the forehand side up) with an extremely fast topspin motion. It's a relatively new serve, though there are reports of players doing this long ago. It's the fastest serve in table tennis.

Inside-out loop—a sidespin loop where a forehand loop breaks right (for a righty), or (less common) a righty's backhand loop breaks left (also for a righty).

Inverted sponge—The most common racket covering. It consists of a sheet of pimpled rubber on top of a layer of sponge. The pips point inward, so the surface is smooth. This is the opposite of pips-out sponge, where the pips point outward.

ITTF—International Table Tennis Federation. The governing body for table tennis in the world. See www.ittf.com.

Kill shot—See smash.

Let—If play is interrupted for any reason during a rally, a let is called and the point does not count.

Loaded—A ball with a great deal of spin.

Lob—A high defensive return of a smash, usually done with topspin or sidespin.

Long—See Deep.

Long pips—A type of pips-out rubber where the pips are long and thin and bend on contact with the ball. It returns the ball with whatever spin was on it, and is very difficult to play against if you are not used to it.

Loop—A heavy topspin shot, done forehand or backhand, and the dominant shot at the higher levels. Most players either specialize in looping or in handling the opponent's loop.

Looper—A style of play where the primary shot is the loop.

Match—Usually best three out of five games to 11. Sometimes matches are best two out of three (rarely in tournaments) or best four out of seven games, also to 11.

Middle (deep balls)—On deep balls, a ball to the middle goes to the opponent's crossover point between forehand and backhand, usually around the elbow.

Middle (short balls)—On short balls, a ball to the middle of the table, near the doubles line.

Neutral racket—The racket is neither open nor closed, and so is perpendicular to the floor.

Open racket—If the hitting surface of the racket is aimed upwards, with the top edge leaning towards you, it is open.

Pendulum serve—The most common serve at higher levels. The serve is done on the forehand side, with the racket tip down, and the racket moving from right to left (for a right-hander). (See also Reverse Pendulum serve.)

Penholder—A type of grip used mostly by Asians. It generally gives a strong forehand but sometimes a more awkward backhand if done conventionally instead of with a reverse penhold backhand.

Pips—The small conical bits of pimpled rubber that cover a sheet of table tennis rubber.

Pips-out—A type of racket covering. It consists of a sheet of pips-out rubber on top of a layer of sponge. The pips point outward, the opposite of inverted. Also called short pips.

Playing surface—The top of the table, including the edges.

Push—A backspin return of backspin.

Pushblocker—A player who returns nearly everything with quick, dead blocks, even against backspin, usually with long pips (often without sponge), sometimes with hardbat or antispin.

Racket—The blade plus covering.

Racket hand—The hand that holds the racket.

Rally—The hitting of the ball back and forth, commencing with the serve and ending when a point is won.

Rating—A number that is assigned to all tournament players after their first tournament. The better the player the higher the rating should be. The range is from just above 0 to nearly 3000. See USATT ratings.

Rating events—An event in a tournament where to be eligible you must be rated under a specified number.

Receive—The return of a serve.

Reverse pendulum serve—Like a pendulum serve, except the racket moves from left to right (for a right-hander), creating the reverse type of spin. This is one of the most popular serves at the higher levels. (See also Pendulum serve.)

Reverse penhold backhand—A backhand by a penhold player where he hits with the opposite side of the racket rather than using the same side for forehand and backhand (i.e. a conventional penhold backhand). Most top penholders now play their backhands this way as it gives a stronger backhand attack, though it leaves the player weaker in the middle and often isn't as good for blocking.

Rubber—The racket covering. Sometimes refers only to the rubber on top of a sponge base.

Rubber cleaner—Used to keep the surface of inverted rubber clean.

Sandwich rubber—A sponge base covered by a sheet of rubber with pips, with the pips pointing either in or out. If pointed in, it is inverted sponge. If pointed out, it is pips-out sponge.

Seemiller grip—A grip that is often used in the United States. Named after five-times U.S. National Champion Dan Seemiller, who first developed it. Most coaches consider it an inferior grip, and outside the U.S. it is almost unheard of. Also called the American Grip.

Serve—The first shot in a rally, done by the server. It begins with the ball being thrown up from the palm of the hand and struck by the racket.

Shakehands grip—The most popular grip. It gives the best balance of forehand and backhand.

Short—A ball that would bounce twice on the opponent's side of the table if given the chance.

Short pips—See pips-out.

Shovel serve—A forehand serve where the racket is almost parallel to the floor. By pointing the racket tip slightly up or down the server can create serves with sidespin in either direction.

Sidespin—a type of spin that makes the ball jump sideways when it hits the opponent's racket.

Sidespin block—A block with sidespin.

Smash—A putaway shot. Ball is hit with enough speed so opponent cannot make a return.

Smother kill—To smash right off the bounce. Usually done against a lob.

Spin—The rotation of the ball.

Sponge—The bouncy rubber material used in sandwich rubber. It is used under a sheet of rubber with pips. It revolutionized the game and ended the hard rubber age in the 1950's. Inverted sponge dominates the game, especially at the higher levels.

Strategic thinking—Finding a way to improve your game so you win more in the future.

Strawberry flip (or flick)—A wristy backhand return of a short ball that's sort of a mini-loop, with topspin and sidespin, with racket moving from left to right (for a righty). Against a sidespin serve, you would mostly do this when you can go with the spin, i.e. against a backhand sidespin-type serve between two righties. This is a relatively rare and difficult shot, meaning the surprise factor if you learn it is high. Most players and coaches probably haven't even heard of this shot. (Why is it called a Strawberry flip? Because it's the opposite of a Banana Flip, and another fruit name was needed! It was named this by Stefan Feth.)

Stroke—Any shot used in the game, including the serve.

Tactical thinking—Finding a way to win a given match.

Time-out—During a match, each player is allowed a single one-minute time-out. This allows the player to rest, clear his mind, think about tactics, or talk to a coach.

Topspin—A type of spin used on most aggressive shots, with an extreme amount being used in the loop shot. When you topspin the ball, the top of the ball moves away from you. Topspin pulls the ball down.

Tomahawk serve—A forehand serve with the racket tip up, and the racket moving from left to right (for a right-hander).

Tweeny serve—Another name for a half-long serve.

Two-step footwork—A popular style of footwork.

Umpire—The official who keeps score and enforces rules during a match.

Underspin—See backspin.

USATT—USA Table Tennis. The governing body for table tennis in the United States. Until the 1990s it was the United States Table Tennis Association (USTTA). See www.usatt.org.

USATT Ratings—A rating system run by USA Table Tennis. Beginners start off somewhere under 1000. An average club player is around 1500, an average tournament player around 1800, a "master" player is 2000 or perhaps 2200, U.S. team members are in the 2500-2750 range, and the best players in the world approach 2900. Roughly speaking, a player will upset a player rated 100 points higher about one out of six times.

U.S. Table Tennis Hall of Fame—Each year the U.S. Table Tennis Hall of Fame Committee inducts players and contributors into the U.S. Table Tennis Hall of Fame, with 138 members as of January, 2013. See http://usatt-halloffame.org

Volley—To hit the ball before it bounces on your side of the table. It results in an immediate loss of the point.

Notes

Notes

Notes

Notes

Notes

Notes

International Table Tennis Skills DVD
Over Two Hours of Action
NOW Available at
www.samsondubina.com

Samson Dubina
TABLE TENNIS ACADEMY
SamsonDubina.com

The Samson Dubina Table Tennis Academy is dedicated to bringing the Olympic sport of table tennis to a new level in Ohio through professional coaching, elite tournaments, world class equipment, and promoting sportsmanship on and off the court. Go to **www.samsondubina.com** for table tennis equipment, table tennis news, and FREE coaching advice.

UNLEASHING GOD'S TRUTH ONE VERSE AT A TIME

THE MACARTHUR STUDY BIBLE

NEW KING JAMES VERSION

Signature Series

Table Tennis Tactics for Thinkers

By Larry Hodges
USATT Hall of Famer
and National Coach

TABLE
TENNIS
TIPS
Larry Hodges
Three years and
150 online tips now
compiled in one volume!

PROFESSIONAL TABLE TENNIS COACHES HANDBOOK

How YOU can become a Professional Coach!

By Larry Hodges
USATT Certified National Coach & Hall of Famer
www.TableTennisCoaching.com

Table Tennis Tales & Techniques

by Larry Hodges
USA Table Tennis Hall of Famer

STEPS to SUCCESS ACTIVITY SERIES

TABLE TENNIS

Steps to Success

LARRY HODGES

in cooperation with
United States Table Tennis Association

Printed in Great Britain
by Amazon